Guide to Licensing and Acquiring Electronic Information

Stephen Bosch
Patricia A. Promis
Chris Sugnet

with contributions by Trisha Davis

ALCTS Acquisitions Guides, No. 13
Collection Management and
Development Guides, No. 13

Association for Library Collections & Technical Services,
a division of the American Library Association
Published in cooperation with
The Scarecrow Press, Inc., of Lanham, Maryland
2005

SCARECROW PRESS, INC.

Published in the United States of America
by Scarecrow Press, Inc.
A wholly owned subsidiary of
The Rowman & Littlefield Publishing Group, Inc.
4501 Forbes Boulevard, Suite 200, Lanham, Maryland 20706
www.scarecrowpress.com

PO Box 317
Oxford
OX2 9RU, UK

British Library Cataloguing in Publication Information Available

Library of Congress Cataloging-in-Publication Data

Bosch, Stephen.
  Guide to licensing and acquiring electronic information / Stephen Bosch,
Patricia A. Promis, Chris Sugnet.
    p. cm. — (ALCTS acquisitions guides ; no. 13) (Collection management and
development guides ; no. 13)
  Includes bibliographical references and index.
  ISBN 0-8108-5259-4 (pbk. : alk. paper)
    1. Acquisition of electronic information resources—United States. 2. Copyright—
Electronic information resources—United States. 3. License agreements.
4. Libraries and electronic publishing. I. Promis, Patricia. II. Sugnet, Chris.
III. Title. IV. Series. V. Series : Acquisitions guidelines ; no. 13.
  Z689 .A2746 1973 no. 13   [Z692.C65]
  025.2 s—dc22   [025.2/   2004028666

∞™ The paper used in this publication meets the minimum requirements of
American National Standard for Information Sciences—Permanence of Paper
for Printed Library Materials, ANSI/NISO Z39.48-1992.
Manufactured in the United States of America.

Contents

Acknowledgments

We would like to thank Ken Bierman, director of knowledge access management at the University of Nevada Las Vegas Libraries, for his editorial assistance and Trisha Davis for her contributions to this book.

I

Introduction

The acquisition and selection of materials published in electronic format for library collections is a complex process applied to a marketplace that is rapidly changing. The multiplicity of new terms used to describe information in electronic form, including *digital information* and *remotely served information*, is indicative of a period of rapid change. For purposes of consistency, this book will refer to "electronic products" as all digitally based information regardless of access mechanism.

Electronic products present many unique challenges. The same content is available in multiple formats from different vendors. The acquisition of these products requires different processing procedures due to the lack of a physical product. New pricing models and options are used, and in most situations there is the need to negotiate license agreements. Technological issues also exist. Does the local information technology (IT) infrastructure support the telecommunications bandwidth needed to offer a product? Does the local system have enough server capacity to handle the expected transactions? Who will be responsible for supplying accurate lists of the customers' current Internet protocol (IP) addresses to the vendor so access can be established and maintained? Who in the organization will provide leadership needed to expand the breadth of knowledge required to effectively select and order these products? In addition to these issues, electronic products introduce new facets to traditional preservation issues and often provide unclear or untested access to perpetual archives.

As librarians offer new services, new materials, and new electronic formats to their clientele, additional budgetary and overhead costs are introduced. The budgetary constraints libraries have been facing for more than a decade are exacerbated by the strategic need to transition into a digital environment while maintaining an up-to-date traditional collection. The fact that many higher-priced titles once purchased as monographs in paper format now must be purchased on an annual basis in electronic format adds to the budgetary difficulties. In addition, many publishers strive to maintain revenue from printed products so they can afford the reengineering necessary to compete in the digital marketplace.

These increased costs fuel a growing need for libraries to budget for simultaneous access to information in several formats. Libraries purchase the print format and then pay either a surcharge or the full price for the digital equivalent, thus negating the reputed cost savings of moving to electronic resources. Solutions such as consortial purchasing may offer cost reductions but often increase the complexity of acquisitions transactions.

The traditional process of ordering and receiving information in various physical formats is being replaced with a process of negotiating remote access to information in electronic format and then monitoring that the information is available to the purchaser's IP range. The acquisition of electronic products requires an entirely different set of considerations than those weighed when material in more traditional formats is selected and purchased. Unlike printed information selection, electronic collections development often requires expertise in the review and negotiation of site licenses; continual awareness of availability of products from alternative suppliers; clear and ongoing communication among consortial partners; technical knowledge to assess different text and image options and maintain Internet addresses; an ability to evaluate a growing variety of pricing options, which may include electronic content bundled with paper and/or MARC records; and processing flexibility to accommodate new editions of essential titles that are suddenly no longer available in print.

Once selection decisions are made, acquisition and maintenance of electronic products often require a parallel workflow to be established. Since publications created or reformatted in electronic form are most likely serial publications with annual maintenance commitments, the impact is greatest on staff who process serials. Now library staff must not only continue to check in and claim paper issues of serials, but also monitor the availability of remotely served electronic products and contact publishers, as well as third-party servers to reestablish access if it is interrupted.

A. Purpose of This Book

The purpose of this book is to provide an overview of the electronic products environment that is pertinent to libraries of all types, a framework to approach the selection and acquisition of these products, and best practices for capitalizing on the transition to electronic products. Like most books, it is not a comprehensive treatise but rather an introduction to the issues and options available to practitioners. References to related information in other publications and resources are provided where appropriate.

B. Definitions and Scope

The materials in electronic format discussed in this book include those that can be viewed and magnetically stored and retrieved with electronic technology and that are available as individual products. All can be manipulated through the use of computers. Examples of these materials are:

- full-text files, such as books, patents, directories, and journals
- numeric data files, such as census or stock market files or the Social Science Data tapes from the Inter-University Consortium for Political and Social Research (ICPSR)
- indexing and abstracting services or similar reference databases stored on servers, CD-ROMs, DVDs, or computer hard drives, or accessed through local area networks (LANs) or the World Wide Web
- software, computer programs, and nonnumeric, machine-readable data files
- videotapes, videodiscs, and video games
- geospatial files from government and commercial sources

This book covers the acquisition process for most of the existing electronic formats presently available to all types of libraries. It also provides information pertinent to the selection and acquisitions process, a glossary of terms commonly used in the library world when referring to electronic materials, and a list of sources that can be consulted for more detailed information. The book also addresses various issues connected to these types of resources, such as copyright concerns, licensing considerations, the needed development of appropriate standards, prices, and establishing LANs.

It is important to note from the outset that this book is written primarily for libraries that are educational in mission. Most items discussed will be of value to all libraries. Corporate libraries, however, are not covered by all the educational copyright allowances provided in the "fair use" doctrine of U.S. copyright law, and they may need to reinterpret some issues concerning copyrights, licenses, and lease agreements.

II

Formats of Electronic Information: Discussion of Material Types

This chapter briefly describes the various forms of electronic products routinely purchased by libraries and notes the opportunities and challenges posed by each type. Most products on the market today are available directly from the content producer or from intermediary parties such as vendors, distributors, library consortia, or regional networks. Generally speaking, selecting and purchasing any electronic product through a second party offers advantages and disadvantages. Often, the acquisition of an item is governed by a license agreement with the publisher. If modification or clarification of the agreement is necessary, it may be easier to deal directly with the publisher.

A. Electronic Journals

Many publishers of journals and magazines are developing electronic formats and are offering both paper and digital alternatives. Some are establishing new journals and others are offering their traditional paper titles in electronic form only. Electronic journals offer enormous opportunities and some significant challenges.

A positive aspect of selecting an electronic journal is the obvious advantage of its multiple-use availability, which contrasts with the limitations of a paper copy that at any given time can be in use, missing, vandalized, worn out, or off to the commercial bindery. Add to this the immediacy of access all day, every day—24-7, and the probability that off-site users can gain remote access through proxy servers. Electronic journals also often offer powerful keyword and other indexing access points and cross-linking between article citations in electronic indexes and the full text of the cited article. Another promising aspect is possibility for cross-linking between footnoted citations in an electronic journal article and electronic forms of the cited articles on the Internet.

Another advantage of electronic journals is the reduced staff time needed to check in, claim, and process physical items and the reduction in commercial binding and replacement costs. However, as the shift to electronic journals accelerates, reductions in staffing for processing print collections will be offset by the need to license, link, and perform other management activities. In the print environment, serials check-in requires low-level staffing while the equivalent work in the electronic environment is much more complex. It is fair to state that the level of complexity is rising as work shifts from checking in and claiming paper journal issues to maintaining access to electronic journals. Additionally, a decision matrix or an electronic resource management system, and/or link-resolver systems have to be purchased or developed to maintain access to numerous publishers' websites and third-party aggregator servers. A management system helps track license terms that impact remote access. Some systems manage electronic holdings, and a link-resolver establishes and maintains "click through" links between journal citations used in indexing and abstracting tools and the full-text articles subscribed to by the library. This process may involve not only acquisitions staff but also systems, collection development, and cataloging staff as well.

Although collecting meaningful journal use statistics is theoretically easier in the electronic environment, the multiplicity of approaches used by publishers to maintain server statistics and the difficulty in defining what constitutes a meaningful use are short-term obstacles. These issues will be resolved as standards are developed and adopted and as the market matures.

Getting a clear focus on the challenging aspects of electronic journals is more difficult because the issues are numerous and are complicated by the fact that they are available in a number of formats. Libraries can subscribe to electronic journals individually, purchase them as part of a package of subscriptions from a given publisher, or obtain them as value-added content in what are termed "aggregator" full-text products. The aggregator products offer content from numerous journals from many different publishers. Because publishers can drop any journal midstream and also tend to eliminate content as it gets older, they are often the most problematic for assuring "cover-to-cover" access to a given journal for specific years. However, they also represent affordable alternatives to journal subscriptions for many smaller libraries and are very popular "all-in-one" gateways to journal literature for undergraduate use. Depending on how a library subscribes to journals, the various challenges outlined below may or may not impact how and how quickly it decides to move into the electronic journal arena.

One big challenge a library faces if it switches to electronic-only journals is losing local control over archival copies. Although publishers routinely offer some assurances of "perpetual access" to electronic archives in their licenses, the assurances have not been tested to any meaningful extent. Another issue is the lack of a single, broadly accepted format for electronic archives. Because important archival issues such as these are unresolved, many libraries choose to retain subscriptions to paper as a backup, thus canceling out any potential cost savings offered by electronic journals.

Another challenge inherent in the move to licensed electronic content is the shift away from the general principle of fair use offered by U.S. copyright law, which protects the sharing of articles in paper journals and is the linchpin of the interlibrary loan (ILL) system. The ability to share electronic copies of journal articles is dependent on license terms allowing such activity. This issue will be examined in more depth in the licensing chapter of this book.

B. Electronic Books

Monographs in electronic format present many of the same advantages and challenges as electronic journals. While journals represent a much more vigorous segment of electronic publishing, monographs are now being offered in dual paper and digital versions and in some cases only in electronic format. Generally, whenever a monograph is either converted from paper into a digital format or created as an original electronic product, the reader is presented with either a static image file (PDF for example) or a text file with embedded images. The latter can usually be indexed by keyword and searched. Many electronic monographs are available on the Internet now, although some titles are still available electronically only as CD-ROMs.

The e-books' market for libraries is rapidly changing, and we expect current models to be quickly augmented by new products. This will parallel the change from scanning original paper copies, basically reformatting works designed for the print environment, to creating electronic books as the primary product with paper as the secondary market. A number of efforts are under way to provide free public access to scholarly books, ranging from the venerable Project Gutenberg to California University Press's new electronic collection of hundreds of previously published titles. To get a feel for titles that libraries can purchase or link to for free, one can scan university library websites with extensive listings, like the University of Texas at Austin site, www.lib.utexas.edu/books/etext.html.

To better understand the issues evolving in the commercial market, the website for the Society for Scholarly Publishing, www.sspnet.org, is a good place to start. Standards are one of the key obstacles being addressed now because of ongoing, inherent problems with books coming out in proprietary formats. Currently, Microsoft and Adobe are the primary choices, but libraries need to be aware of the Open Archive Initiative and also work underway in the commercial market, exemplified by the Open Ebook Format (www.openbook.org).

Creating books originally in electronic format opens great opportunities for multimedia applications and built-in linking. The availability of remotely served, multimedia-linked titles will change the concept of "monograph" as used in library collection development. Libraries will obtain many titles through annual maintenance commitments, and the acquisitions process will become similar to that of serial publications.

In the remote-access arena, OCLC's NetLibrary is perhaps the largest and best-known provider of copyrighted monographs in electronic form. They have purchased rights to thousands of newer titles from well-known trade and scholarly presses. They started by converting original paper copies by scanning them and then began accepting electronic texts directly from some of their partners. Several library consortia have purchased thousands of titles for member access directly over the Internet. Regardless of whether a library purchases collections or individual titles, users can view a small portion of a work, access an entire work for a brief period of time, or check out the work according to a circulation period designed by the library. Although NetLibrary was a pioneer in the transition to electronic books, the financial problems associated with its business model may force other would-be electronic book publishers to look for radically different models.

Other ways to provide access to copyrighted e-books include direct purchase of remote access to electronic texts from a publisher and purchase of a site license to entire subject-focused collections. Several companies that offer traditional book approval plans have announced availability of electronic alternatives, which can be selected title by title or profiled for automatic purchase.

Entering MARC records into the OPAC for any electronic books in the collection is generally regarded as astute marketing, thus presenting patrons with OPAC query responses that indicate all resources available to them. These records can sometimes be purchased from the supplier of the electronic books and should be negotiated as part of the purchase if they are available. It is good to keep the costs of bibliographic access in mind for even the so-called "free" electronic books. These monographs are sometimes supplied in electronic form because the paper copy has already been purchased, the e-books are an experiment by the publisher, they are out of copyright protection (e.g., Project Gutenberg), or they were created for a nonprofit entity that holds the copyright specifically for free public use.

Another area to pay particular attention when shopping for electronic books is file format. Public libraries are especially likely to enter into purchasing arrangements where format standards become a major issue. In today's marketplace, a variety of handheld readers are in use. E-books formatted for one reader may not be usable on a competitor's machine. Libraries that invest in readers should understand the risks of proprietary formatting and might be wise to consider them only as short-term access mechanisms and thus considered as disposable technology rather than permanent additions to their collections. There is a movement toward file format standardization called the Open e-Book (OEB) Publication Structure that uses public domain coding such as HTML and XML. Purchasing only OEB-compliant devices may be advisable.

The bottom line is to maintain awareness of the changing market in electronic monographs by monitoring online discussion groups, talking with colleagues, and making a practice of arranging new product demonstrations.

A library may need to address the following selection and acquisition issues:

- How is selection done if the entire collection is not purchased?
- What is the subject mix, availability of reference titles, and chronological currency?
- How is use measured?
- Should titles be duplicated in paper?
- Should multiple copies of e-books be purchased outright or leased for a period of time?
- Should access to multiple copies be acquired in response to use?
- Should an approval plan be established through a traditional book jobber that allows a profile to select electronic copies?
- Can some titles be selected for permanent access while others (software manuals, etc.) are selected for specified periods and then weeded?
- What are the archival issues and warranties for perpetual access?

C. DVDs and Videotapes

Standard educational, public-service, and commercially produced videotapes and discs (digital versatile or DVD) are available from a wide variety of vendors, including some that are currently used by acquisitions departments for book purchases. Not all video products are available from all vendors, and it will be necessary to directly order some titles from specialty vendors or the publishers. A DVD can hold significantly more data than a CD-ROM. A standard DVD can hold approximately fourteen times as much data as a standard CD, and a high-density or hDVD can hold four times the amount of a standard DVD. Information is stored on CDs and DVDs using the same basic technology and materials. However, DVDs require a red laser to read a dual layer of encoded pits on the disc; CDs use an infrared laser to read a single layer. The DVD is the reason that LaserDisc analog technology has been abandoned by the entertainment industry. Although some libraries may still have products available on laser disc, player availability will eventually be a problem as it becomes obsolete and too expensive to maintain. Just as CDs have become the most popular format for music, DVDs are becoming the most popular format for video products.

Librarians need to be aware of the practice called "regional locking," in which DVDs are encoded to play only on machines purchased in a specific geographic area or country. Players can be modified, but at the risk of voiding warranties. The best approach may be to purchase only DVDs manufactured in North America until (and if) this practice is discontinued. Another security practice that librarians need to monitor affects the ability to make archival copies. Although machines are available to copy DVDs and licenses may allow copying, many DVD publishers employ an encoded content protection system that blocks copying. Circumvention, without explicit right to do so, violates the Digital Millennium Copyright Act (DMCA) and could have serious legal outcomes.

The acquisition process for videos differs little from that for printed materials except that rights and pricing structures vary. Specialized academic/educational videos may be much more expensive than those produced for the commercial market. When first released, popular commercial titles are relatively expensive, ranging from fifty to one hundred dollars. Unlike book prices, however, prices for videos fall dramatically soon after release when the market has become saturated. The prices and services offered by vendors will vary, and it pays to compare costs and benefits. There is a growing "used" trade, but it is not well organized at this time. The purchase of used videotapes or DVDs as a regular approach to collection development is not recommended for circulating collections because previous wear creates a use and preservation problem. DVDs offer a better solution to preservation concerns and better image resolution so the retention of videotapes by libraries will probably become an issue except for those specialized subjects that will not be released on DVD.

More and more frequently, libraries are offered gift collections that may include home recordings of commercially produced materials. The copyright laws do not allow public use of materials recorded for private use. These gifts should not be accepted. Gifts of privately produced home videos (without any commercial content) can be accepted based on the library's collection development policy. Gifts of commercially produced videotapes fall under the same guidelines as those purchased by the library and are acceptable.

D. Video Games (Instructional and Recreational)

Libraries are a secondary market for video games, which are designed primarily for personal use. In general, these materials are software stored on DVDs or cartridges designed to operate on one video game system only.

Hardware for game systems usually includes the video machine that handles the game discs or cartridges, controllers (joysticks, etc.), and a video monitor. While some sophisticated games interact with video images from videodiscs, DVDs, or CD-ROMs and may require the additional use of these items, other video games are actually software programs that run on PCs. The latter are products that should be treated as software. Popular video games are available from the same vendors that handle videotapes and software. Contacting vendors or mail-order houses that specialize in computer software to obtain these materials is often the most cost effective.

The commercial video game market has been dominated by proprietary concerns. Until recently, the leading video game company had forced the publishers of its game cartridges to incorporate a proprietary design into its products. The effect has been that games from one company work on only that company's game system. For example, games that run on Nintendo machines cannot be used on Sony PlayStation systems and vice versa. Thus, when purchasing games, one should be careful to check which systems can use them.

Video game technology is rapidly evolving. The graphics and functionality available in game systems have greatly improved as the cost of basic computer chips has come down. As the technology changes and improves, public pressure will force libraries to update their game collections with media (such as DVDs) for new game machines. Because old games often will not play on new machines, before long a collection of video games can become obsolete.

E. CD-ROM

CD-ROM is the acronym for "compact disc read-only memory." This technology relies on the use of laser beam light to reflect off patterns embedded in a polycarbonate disc. The reflected beam of light is then "read" by the machine and turned into information or images. A standard 4.75-inch CD-ROM disc can contain hundreds of megabytes of computer-accessible information. In addition to computer-accessible information, this technology can encode moving video images, still-frame graphics, and digital and analog audio. These formats can be combined on a single disc to produce full multimedia applications. Audio CDs can be played on a variety of systems including computers but do not require the use of computers. Currently, most data-oriented CD-ROM applications use personal computers equipped with a CD-ROM drive or player. Accessing information stored on more advanced CD-ROM technology requires the use of a computer with a special optical (CD-ROM) drive. CD-ROM players vary from units that can read one disc at a time to units that can contain and access multiple discs (a jukebox for CDs). Don't assume if you have an optical drive that it will work for all formats of CD, CD-ROM, and DVD.

CD-ROM drives that have the capability not only to read but also to record are on the market. CD-R (CD-Recordable) drives use CD-R discs, which are WORM (Write Once, Read Multiple) media and play just like standard CDs. CD-R discs can be accessed with a standard CD player, but the discs, once recorded, cannot be reused. A related CD recording technology called CD-Rewritable (CD-RW) allows you to write to both CD-R and CD-RW discs and to erase and reuse CD-RW discs. CD-RW discs do not work in all players, however.

Another optional component of drive hardware that works in tandem with built-in software is the ability to write MPEG-1 Audio Layer 3 (Mp3) sound files to a CD. Mp3 is the sound format associated with MPEG, the most-used digital video format. It is a compression format that removes sound bites inaudible to the human ear, saving large amounts of file storage space. New CD-R and CD-RW drives may come with Mp3 compatibility.

In addition to drive hardware, software is required to make information encoded in a CD-ROM retrievable. Some drive products include the software as part of a package; others require the purchase and installation of additional software. Before purchasing an information product in CD-ROM format, be sure to carefully analyze system requirements to determine the type of hardware needed. When ordering, it may be necessary to state which version (IBM, Apple, etc.) is required on the purchase order.

F. Software

Computers cannot operate without some form of software (software being, essentially, the group of instructions that directs computers to perform tasks). An immense variety of software is available in the marketplace. However, a significant portion of software products falls outside of the collecting interests of most libraries. In particular, libraries rarely collect software that provide specific applications, such as those used to support medical and dental offices, banks, retail sales, etc. Libraries frequently purchase software as a value-added activity or a public service, allowing patrons on-site use, but the purchase is not intended for "collecting" purposes. Software can be classified in the following basic types:

Operating systems. This type of software, including Microsoft Windows and UNIX, provides a computer with basic instructions for storing, formatting, and retrieving information. Although it controls basic computer operations, such as formatting disks, creating directories, and copying files, most users will require other software applications to make full use of a computer. Operating systems can perform many functions of application programs (see below), but they require a great deal of programming skill on the part of a user.

Programming tools and languages. Simply stated, programming tools such as Visual Basic and C+ are languages understood by computers that allow users to create their own specific computer applications. They differ from application programs, such as Microsoft Word (see below), in that the latter represents a prepackaged set of instructions in a particular computer language. Programming tools are generally used to develop specific computer functions not enabled by prepackaged software. Users of such tools must have specific knowledge of the tools themselves as well as an extensive understanding of computer programming.

Application programs. Application programs comprise the largest portion of the commercial software market. Within this group, a wide variety is available: personal applications, such as spreadsheets, word processing systems, database management systems, and desktop publishing systems; research tools for sophisticated statistical analysis and modeling; educational programs that provide computer-assisted instruction; business-oriented software for such uses as accounting, data management, and computer-aided design/computer-aided manufacturing (CAD/CAM); and entertainment software, including arcade-type video games (see related section above). Application programs are generally of greatest interest to library users as they enable a computer to perform sophisticated operations without a great deal of user training.

Shareware. This category of software is a subgroup of the basic classifications already described. Shareware is available in the public domain and has few restrictions for its use. Unless it is copyrighted, it can be copied at will and distributed without the normal limitations of commercial products. Publishers of copyrighted shareware rely on free copying to market their products and often require users to register and pay a small fee. Sometimes such payments entitle users to future upgrades, improved documentation, and product support.

Datasets. Datasets are computer software programs that are informational in nature and generally perform a function. They act on some type of information. Data files represent raw information. In most situations some form of retrieval system or at minimum an operating system will be required to use data files. These files may include numeric data, bibliographic information, or the full text of documents. An example of widely used data sets in the university research environment is remote sensing data from U.S. government satellites.

G. Locally and Remotely Loaded Full-Text Content

During the past few years, libraries have made a substantial shift away from acquiring content in print to providing access via Internet gateways to electronic products stored on remote servers. Traditional reference tools, including indexes and abstracts, have become widely available in electronic format, and library users now prefer to use the electronic versions of most products, especially those that offer full-text and full-image content. Full-text availability is especially prevalent in the science, technology, and medicine (STM) area, having perhaps the highest level of availability at this time, although similar shifts to electronic publication in other subject areas are increasing steadily. In the electronic products' marketplace new players have sprung up quickly, offering monographic and serial content accompanied by value-added tools with which to manipulate it. Whether they will become head-to-head competitors with libraries or symbiotic partners remains unclear. In the meantime, library staff needs to stay aware of the options they provide to users.

As the trend has been to provide access via the Internet to remotely stored and served electronic products, now even the smallest libraries offer access to a significant amount of content that does not reside locally in print or electronic form. Locally served electronic products are becoming increasingly rare. The decision to purchase and locally deliver an electronic product must be based on careful consideration of the complexities involved, balancing the full cost to implement the product against the potential service benefits to users. The benefits generally include better response times and system uptime and the archival value of owning the data. However, mounting a major product in a local system is much more expensive due to the prohibitive costs of the product itself and the technology to access it. Although some small bibliographic and full-text databases and locally produced data files may be very cost effective to distribute in a library system, they usually serve only special needs. Through consortial purchasing, the acquisition of databases may be feasible; even so, only large consortia and a few large research libraries find it reasonable to mount such products in local systems.

A library must perform careful analysis of all the costs involved to judge the cost-effectiveness of purchasing and mounting an electronic information product online. The library should include in its calculations the increased system capacity required to store, process, and retrieve the data; the publisher's actual sale price for the data; and costs relating to the retrieval software, data processing to conform to local system requirements, storage in the local system, maintenance and future updates, and specialized staff to do all the technical work.

Regardless of whether the electronic product is stored on a local or a remote server, the associated costs of maintaining and upgrading local servers, networks, and workstations can become a significant portion of a library's budget. Annual maintenance contracts alone can be prohibitively expensive unless a library shares costs with its parent institution or consortium members. Hardware and software upgrades and enhanced peripherals, such as scanners and color printers, are also part of the ongoing expense. However, as great as the expenses may be, a library must weigh them against the improvements in patron access; the savings gained by no longer purchasing the information in paper, CD-ROM, or DVD format; and the staff time saved by no longer handling the receiving and processing of the physical items for the collection.

III

Selection

Selection of electronic resources can no longer be done in isolation. Although it ultimately must remain within the selectors' realm of responsibilities, selectors have to work in collaboration or consultation with other experts in the library before making a decision or recommendation. Aside from subject content, selectors need to consider equipment specifications, software compatibility, and the budgetary implications that go beyond the print format's traditional budget lines when considering the purchase of electronic resources. Because of this, the selection process should involve subject specialists, reference librarians, network specialists, and technical staff. In addition, selectors of electronic resources must be properly trained and their training must be an ongoing endeavor. They must also be well informed of new trends and developments in their field(s) of expertise to bring the necessary technological advances to their users. Selectors play a crucial role in the development of the "electronic" library.

Users' demands and expectations have already grown tremendously and will continue to grow. The electronic environment has made users accustomed to immediate responses to their information needs with minimal searching. Selectors therefore must be aware of the demands of their primary clientele and the type of resource and formats that are preferred.

A. Selection Criteria

1. Policy Issues

a. A sound and up-to-date collection development policy addressing the needs of the users served by the library should remain the basis for its selection of materials, regardless of the format. A policy specifically addressing electronic resources should be in place and in alignment with the general collection development policy.

b. In addition, it is recommended that libraries have clear procedures that specify who is responsible for selecting electronic resources, who should be consulted during the selection process, and what elements of the product must be evaluated before decisions are made.

c. Libraries should regularly evaluate and revise their selection procedures and criteria. Since the elements affecting a selection decision will vary depending on the format under consideration, it is recommended that libraries establish a separate procedure for each format (Internet, CD-ROM, video, etc.).

d. Libraries should address the constraints and demands imposed by the license agreement at this stage in the process.

e. Libraries should have in place a clear definition of the primary and secondary clientele they serve and should consider that clientele during the selection process.

f. Current use and demand for the printed version of an item should be a sound indicator of the need for the electronic version.

g. Libraries should consider the reputation of any publisher they intend to patronize. A list of current customers may be available from the publisher to obtain information about the product.

h. Several review sources provide extensive evaluation of electronic products and should also be consulted. For a detailed list of these resources, see "Review Sources" under "Additional Resources" at the end of this book.

i. Libraries should compare the usefulness of the electronic product versus the printed counterpart.

j. A product's technical capability is an important preservation concern and needs to be considered during the selection stage. Is the medium technically robust and long lasting or fragile and short lived?

k. Libraries should pay special attention to the cost/benefit tradeoff between the electronic data's immediate usefulness and potential degradation.

2. Service Issues

a. The selection criteria should be in alignment with the library's mission and its general plan for information technology.

b. Libraries should evaluate public service staffing and training levels for electronic resources in light of the additional services the resources make available to users.

c. Online help and tutorials should be available for each electronic product.

d. Information and tutorials should be easy to use, accurate, and up to date.

e. Libraries should assess the implications for current library staffing and training brought about by cataloging and processing materials in various electronic formats.

f. Libraries should evaluate the effectiveness of search engines for retrieving electronic data.

g. Libraries should consult product demonstrations, reviews, and evaluations.

h. Libraries should take into account the availability of printing facilities and costs.

3. Technical Issues

a. First and foremost, libraries should determine whether technical support and maintenance are required.

b. Libraries should evaluate the software, in particular for security and compatibility with existing hardware and software.

c. Hardware issues include reliability, maintenance, compatibility with existing peripherals, and flexibility for networking.

d. Libraries should consider alignment with their existing systems and with the systems used and supported by their parent organizations.

e. Libraries should also evaluate flexibility for growth.

f. Environmental and spatial requirements for equipment and workstations need special attention.

4. Cost Considerations

Selectors have some options for addressing the cost factor. Electronic resources tend to be more expensive than traditional print resources. At the same time, they also offer potential savings in binding costs, shelving space, processing time, maintenance, and staffing. Consortial arrangements are a favored option for more expensive items. Sharing the cost with several institutions is efficient and effective. For the most part, the number of consortia to which an institution can belong is unlimited as is the number of institutions with whom it may make cooperative purchasing arrangements.

a. Libraries should consider the preservation benefits of a particular medium.

b. Duplication of information in more than one format usually results in higher costs (including processing, binding, and space). Vendors and publishers are not always receptive when a library switches to the "electronic only" subscription after initially subscribing to the printed format.

c. Cost differentials between aggregators' services and subscriptions through publishers should be reviewed.

d. Libraries should carefully study purchase or lease options.

e. They should take into account additional costs for future updates and upgrades.

f. The price of the product may not reflect additional start-up and maintenance costs.

g. Libraries should explore the availability of discounts for hardware/software packages or bundles associated with the products.

5. Access

Libraries are now more accustomed to dealing with some of the uncertainties of leasing electronic resources as opposed to owning the materials. The constantly changing electronic environment has encouraged the creation of some important initiatives to preserve archives of electronic journals such as JSTOR (Journal Storage) and the Andrew W. Mellon Foundation's e-journal archiving program. More efforts are continuously surfacing. Access to information provided through electronic resources continues to be a concern for libraries. The ideal product will offer easy access to all legitimate users associated with the institution. However, in reality, this is not simple. General access-related issues to consider include:

a. Equal access to all users whether on-site or remote.

b. Authentication for remote users, including distance education students residing in faraway places.

c. Privacy protections for users. Users are entitled to expect that consultations will remain private.

d. The character and quality of the interaction between the end user and the electronic product.

6. Bibliographic Access

a. Libraries should make seamless interfaces from the OPAC to the electronic product. They can establish access from Web pages or bibliographic records or both.

b. OPAC bibliographic entries for electronic products should provide transparent links to the full text of the products if they include full text.

c. Libraries should facilitate the ability to link from resource citations to the corresponding full-text articles. Users want to move from citations directly to content.

d. The product should be able to support most linking systems or at least fit into the local linking systems. As many different approaches are available to provide journal- and article-level linking, assessing products for their ability to support linking features is important. The system in use today may not be the system used tomorrow; therefore, a product's ability to use broad-

based linking features, such as Digital Object Identifiers (DOI, http://www
.doi.org/about_the_doi.html), is a very important consideration.

B. Hardware/Software Considerations

Good electronic information products require the proper interaction of
hardware, telecommunications systems, and software to work well. A library
must consider its local information technology (IT) systems when purchasing these resources. Some electronic information products have specific
hardware and software needs. For example, many products are Web-based.
If a library uses a local system without robust bandwidth, it must carefully
evaluate those Web products that place heavy demands on bandwidth, such
as streaming audio and video or make use of numerous Java applets. Although hardware and software selection issues are treated separately in this
section, both are usually addressed during a single selection decision. Such
a decision might involve input from several areas potentially affected by the
acquisition of the product—including systems, collection management, technical services, and public services—but ultimately someone must make the
decision to purchase or not.

Although most products have a great deal of flexibility, sometimes no real
choice exists among IT support options, as some products work with only
certain software and hardware packages or configurations. It is important to
determine if a particular item can be supported locally prior to purchase. The
key is to examine local needs first, then find the best options. Trials are always a good way to determine if local systems and an electronic information
product make a good fit. Including remote users in product evaluations is
also important as they may have unique needs not immediately apparent to
evaluators in the library. The prepurchase evaluation for any electronic information product should look at a variety of factors—including local hardware, the computer terminals or Web appliances providing in-house access,
local Web browsers, local networks, Internet service providers (ISPs), and
the website itself—to determine if the product is a good choice for the local
IT environment.

1. Software Selection Considerations

Software performs the basic function of providing the link between a computer system's hardware and an electronic information product. It can com-
bine Web access with a search engine and supporting data, or it can allow
users to manipulate their own data. An example of the former is search software that presents structured commands for searching databases from different sources, such as the products offered by SilverPlatter, OCLC's FirstSearch,

or Ovid. Examples of the latter are word processors, spreadsheets, and Web page development tools that are now commonly available in computer labs and information commons.

Software is available from a variety of sources. It can be purchased directly from the publisher or through vendors. System search engines are only available directly from the publisher or information provider. They are frequently bundled with a database or full-text product for free. In such cases, prepurchase evaluation of the search engine will overlap with database selection. Sometimes, however, search engines must be purchased. For many commercial software products, such as word processors, prices will vary widely depending on where they are purchased and the entity making the purchase. National chains generally are cheaper than small, local retail computer stores, and mail order vendors are cheaper than both. Some software is available to libraries at special educational discounts, which can greatly reduce the cost. If multiple copies are going to be purchased, purchasing a site license can be cost effective. These licenses generally allow an organization a certain number of copies of the software to be distributed internally at a cost much lower than purchasing individual copies (for further discussion of licenses, see chapter V, Licensing). When searching for a software source, all of these options should be explored. Because some institutions have purchased broad site licenses for certain types of commercial software, contact the systems office to determine if any software is available through a site license before making software purchases.

An integral part of the software purchase decision process is an assessment of the IT environment where the product will be used. A library should consider environmental issues, such as basic hardware requirements and whether the software will be used in a mainframe, personal computer, or a network before ordering an item. The license agreement and the cost of software may vary if the product is intended to function in a network. If it is intended to circulate, the library should make sure the license agreement governing the item's use does not place restrictions on its circulation. For instance, if the library does not circulate master copies and a product's license agreement forbids copying, it would be unable to circulate copies of the product. Contacting the publisher and renegotiating the standard license agreement's terms for use of a product may be necessary to ensure that the product's intended use is in full compliance. For an in-depth discussion of the issues involved in the selection and circulation of software see *Software for Patron Use in Libraries*, edited by Denise M. Beaubien, A. L. Primack, and C. Seale.

In addition to the basic question of functionality with the local system, a library should consider other critical factors when evaluating a software product. These factors include:

a. User interface. Evaluation of the user interface should cover overall ease in using the software. Is the screen design intuitive or in other words, does the screen display options and information in areas where regular users would expect to find them? Can users easily navigate from task to task? Are the main features of the software evident from the initial user screens?

b. User support. The evaluation of user support should include a review of the overall usefulness of the online documentation and help screens as well as the availability of free online user-support services or toll-free telephone support with extended hours. A library should check with a product's current customers about support services because when users contact the help desks, response time can be very slow.

c. Searching capabilities. When considering search engines, a library should also evaluate the availability of the following:

- different levels of user interfaces (for example, interfaces for beginners and advanced users)
- Boolean and keyword or relational searching, subject searching using a controlled vocabulary
- searching with truncated words
- the ability to store and reuse searches

The response time for different types of searches is a critical factor, as is the usefulness of the introductory instructional documentation. Other factors that a library should evaluate when purchasing software include:

- the library's ability to provide local instruction and user support
- the reliability of the software (e.g., can users easily crash it)
- the compatibility of the software with the current hardware environment
- the general level of user sophistication

The selection of any type of software should be based on criteria similar to those that govern selection of print materials and should fall within the general guidelines for collection development and provision of information resources. However, the users' needs should be the paramount concern when selecting software. Money spent on software that no one will use right away is likely wasted since the shelf life of most software is very short. The purchase decision therefore should not be based on a possibility of future use.

In addition to its general selection criteria, a library must also address other special considerations as part of the electronic information product selection process. If purchasing highly specialized software, the library should first select the software, then choose hardware that can run the software. This applies to such products as geographic information system (GIS) software, which requires special hardware configurations and high-end desktop computers to display and manipulate the geospatial data that often require a plotter to print the data.

The idea of selecting software first, then selecting hardware often breaks down, however, due to the wide variety of available software and heavy investment in the local IT infrastructure that new software products may require. Purchase and maintenance of new hardware and/or operating systems can incur significant costs both financially and in required staff time learning to operate the new system. Therefore, reconfiguring local networks to accommodate every new product is not feasible. Rather, a library's general hardware environment and the needs of its clients or patrons determine the types of software that should be selected. For example, elementary and secondary schools and users needing high-end audio or graphic applications may operate in a hardware environment dominated by Apple computers. In such cases, the software selection should be compatible with the hardware environment. In cases where very specific software is required, the need to match software with hardware becomes critical.

Beyond the hardware environment, of key importance is the software's ability to do what the library needs it to do. A software package may not necessarily be able to do something specific if the publisher's documentation or product reviews do not describe that capability. If in doubt, contact the publisher. Another consideration is how well the software can perform, which involves response time, ease of use, quality of documentation, output—both printed and downloaded, the volume of information it can handle, and its ability to accept information from other sources. These criteria generally apply to software programs. Data files have a different set of considerations that includes the format, structure, and organization of the data; the ability to search and retrieve the data; the ease of use; and the quality of the documentation.

Cost is another necessary selection criterion. Electronic information product pricing is much more complicated than print material pricing—so much so that it could fill another book on its own. Needless to say, many variables affect price. Before purchasing a product, a library should determine whether another less expensive product or a less extensive installation (e.g., fewer users) of the selected product would meet its needs. Software products can perform relatively equally well but vary widely in price. For example, a library might look at two different Web authoring tools that meet its users' needs. One package is basic and much cheaper, while another is designed for Web developers. Both packages would fulfill the library's needs, but one is much less expensive.

As usual, at the retail level the same item is often available for different prices from different sources. To complicate the issue further, the price structure for some products varies according to whether the buyer is an educational institution, whether it will use the product in a network, and whether it purchases a site license for multiple copies of the product. Within a consortium, broad software licenses may already be in place. Sometimes preexisting "state contracts" for software provide deep discounts for the licensed products. All of these considerations should be considered when determining the real cost of the product.

2. Technical Considerations

Technical considerations can be important in selecting electronic information products. Some of these have already been discussed in the preceding section on software selection considerations. When purchasing any IT-related equipment, a library should consult its systems office and be aware that the actual purchase is likely to be performed outside its own acquisitions department. For instance, a purchase involving IT equipment may be budgeted separately and purchased by a unit outside the library's acquisitions department. Information products that come bundled with other hardware or software products could be problematic to units that must divide purchases along strict lines. Before a library makes a final decision to purchase any product, it needs to evaluate the complete IT environment, including the product's hardware and software requirements. Some major points to consider are:

a. What is the current and anticipated demand for the information product?

b. What is the real total cost, including all hardware, support, and product expenses? The overall quality of service is directly related to the amount of money available to support an IT infrastructure capable of providing robust workstations for users.

c. Can the desired information product run on currently available computers?

Related issues include:

a. Overall system compatibility. Some products are designed for one type of computer and will not run on other equipment.

b. Hardware configuration. Do currently available machines have adequate memory, disk storage, and processor speed to support the product?

c. Software platforms. Which software platforms can interface with the selected information product? If Web-based, which browsers and browser versions can support the product?

d. Compatibility with current CD-ROM drives. If the product is a CD-ROM, users may not be able to access the data with satisfactory response time using old drives.

e. Future growth in the size of the product. This may affect the hardware configuration. As the product is updated its size may grow, making it potentially necessary to add more disk storage, memory, routers, updated CD-ROM drives, and other upgrades to maintain the resource. For example, if a system's bandwidth currently can barely provide adequate response time to Web queries, response time could rapidly degrade in the future.

f. Hardware costs. These costs should include the cost of maintenance contracts. The purchase of new hardware may require the following:

- space for the new equipment and additional electrical and telecommunications wiring
- costs for start-up and site preparation
- more staff time for technical and training support
- costs for supplies, such as printers, paper, ink cartridges, disks, and tapes

g. Necessary support. The library will need to decide whether it is willing to supply the necessary hardware.

h. Circulation copies. The library will need to assess the integrity of circulation copies when they are returned. It should provide staff with hardware to screen returned materials for damage or software viruses.

3. Electronic Archives

A library must consider some major issues during the purchase of an electronic information product, which are the continuing ownership rights that are granted and how the product is archived to protect those rights. The library should make sure that the product's license agreement addresses long- and short-term storage. If the product is to be archived locally, the library should identify the resources that can be used to support storage and access. Approaches to archival storage are as numerous as the variety of available products and are continuing to expand.

Because many publishers are offering strong incentives to shift to electronic-only product packages, permanent archiving of owned data has become a closely watched issue. Most publishers will agree to provide an electronic version of subscribed materials on a "permanent" basis but how they will achieve this is often not clearly defined. Some organizations have launched pilot projects to address these issues; the most visible project is one sponsored by the Andrew W. Mellon Foundation. These grants supported the development of archives for electronic scholarly journals and represent successful partnerships between libraries and publishers that provide a viable system for permanently archiving electronic materials.

With the passage of the federal Digital Millennium Copyright Act (DMCA), technical issues concerning the storage of archives and their transference to future versions of software have become murky. The Digital Millennium Copyright Act was enacted in 1998 and at that time was the most comprehensive response to perceived changes needed in U.S. copyright law to address issues associated with digital products. The DMCA brought U.S. copyright law into compliance with the World Intellectual Property Organization

(WIPO) treaties. The DMCA includes provisions concerning the circumvention of copyright protection systems, fair use in a digital environment, and online service provider liability. At first glance, the DMCA would seem to bar any systematic approach to archiving and to refreshing archives when necessary. Although it does allow for exceptions "to achieve interoperability of computer programs," it has not been in effect long enough for it to be tested in court. A body of tort law must evolve to clarify what the law does and does not permit.

Archiving is a major issue, but there are no clear solutions at this time and much to consider. If a library considers it important to obtain archival rights for a product, it should negotiate these rights as part of the licensing process and include a separate clause addressing this. As archival rights may not be granted elsewhere in the license document, it's important to get it in writing. Libraries should be aware of the following considerations:

a. Unless local ownership and control are very important, it is advisable to leave responsibility for providing archival access with the publishers or other third parties. Negotiating this into the license is necessary.

b. Change is inevitable. Any current plan for archiving information and refreshing the archive will need to change as technology changes.

c. Archiving major products, such as e-journal packages and large abstracting and indexing (A&I) databases, should be done only within the allowable contexts of the license agreement. Few individual libraries have assumed responsibility for the cost of archiving, and this would seem to be a good area for cooperation among all stakeholders.

d. Libraries should make archival copies of all data and software (if allowed) and keep backup copies off site. Computer centers are often best equipped to handle this type of storage.

e. Libraries should load software that is regularly used in house onto a disk drive (preferably networked) and store backup copies separately for both the short and long term. This may require the purchase of more expensive site licenses but offers the most effective working environment.

f. Software and other electronic media that circulate should be kept in proper protective containers that prevent damage to the products as they are transported by patrons.

g. Libraries should store software and all other media (such as videotapes) as far as possible from sources of electromagnetic radiation, such as telephones, some theft-detection systems, and even some systems terminals.

h. It is preferable to use CD-ROM drives that require the use of disc carriers (caddies) and to keep the CD-ROM discs in these caddies.

i. The ideal approach to short-term storage of CD-ROMs is to place the discs in a "jukebox" (storage device allowing many CD-ROMs to be housed and used from the single device) and allow access to the information through an individual workstation or a network of workstations. This storage method is expensive because it uses costly hardware and, if access is provided through a local area network (LAN), requires staff to maintain the network. In addition, mounting CD-ROMs in networks usually incurs extra license fees.

j. Libraries should evaluate whether embedded links to other sources that are an integral part of the archive should be maintained. Does the archive need to include content offered by the link? If so, what resources will be committed to ensure that the links connect to the correct content?

The investment involved in providing electronic information is usually substantial, and the need to protect such an investment is obvious. A library needs to work out strategies for storing these products in advance of purchase, implement procedures to provide a safe environment for their storage, and make any necessary transfers of the products to newer storage media. Long-term archival issues should be addressed as part of the purchasing and licensing process. When a library seeks continued ownership, the license agreement should either guarantee perpetual access to the information via remote sites or allow the library to load and display the product from its local systems. The latter option is expensive and would demand an institutional commitment to refresh data as technology changes. If a library stores archival data on tape, the tape may be useless ten years from now if a compatible tape drive is no longer available. As the storage technology changes, the library will need to copy the tape to newer media. In addition, the legal environment is changing. It is important that libraries stay informed and be aware of how these changes might impact current practice.

4. Remote and Networked Access

Libraries make most purchases of electronic products with the intention of providing the broadest possible access to the largest numbers of users. One way they can accomplish this is through networked access via either the Web or local networks. Many complications arise, however, during the purchasing process. As we have already discussed, license wording must allow networked or remote access. In addition, to support remote access, telecommunications systems must be in place. The systems must verify users as legitimate clients of the organization.

User verification or authentication for access to networked resources can be accomplished by several means. A library can control access by use of passwords, verification of Internet protocol (IP) address, or use of a server that checks users' ID numbers or similar identifiers. Access would be accepted for only those users whose information matches records in the server. There are pros and cons for each method. Passwords are difficult to distribute and control in large organizations. Some products do not permit passwords to be embedded in the scripts that allow access without users "seeing" the passwords. IP address verification works by setting up a range of IP addresses with the service provider. The system grants access to users whose IP addresses are in the designated range. This method currently operates well for large systems. But such systems increasingly will have problems due to the growing use of laptop computers in variable locations, since such machines have floating (dynamic) IP addresses. Also, remote users accessing a resource via the Web, using independent ISPs, will not have an identifiable IP address that can be authenticated. Although they may be part of an authorized community, since their Web access may be coming from their own personal ISP, the IP address associated with their activity will not be recognized as part of the registered set of IP addresses. Authentication servers, in conjunction with proxy servers, can address this problem, but user information has to be updated constantly to be accurate. No single solution rises to the top as best practice. A library's local needs should determine which means it uses to verify users and allow them remote or networked access. Some organizations are using combinations of these methods to meet their needs.

Security remains a problem no matter what system is used to verify users. All systems can be hacked. Most licenses for electronic products require swift action to remedy any unauthorized use. If the breach is serious enough, some products immediately close off all access. Computer firewalls can greatly reduce the threat of external hacking into local networks, but even this approach is not foolproof. Providing access to a wide variety of remote users is more difficult if using computer firewalls, but solutions are available. Offering the broadest possible access generally demands the most resources and incurs the greatest cost. Also, the broader the access provided, the higher the risk of unauthorized use.

Another issue that arises with remote access is the need to support users who are off site. Remote users present an infinite variety of computer systems and expertise, but all will expect some level of support. If a library plans to offer remote access, it must develop plans to support the remote users. If it supports distance education programs, this will be especially true. Users will expect assistance with the different Web browsers and software plug-ins in addition to instruction on the use of online information products and up-to-date information when systems go down. The normal practice is to set up e-mail and phone help lines to provide this support.

LANs can be very useful in providing access within an organization. They can offer enhanced security, greatly increase the efficiency of a series of computers and peripherals, and improve access to some online products. LANs can connect users to high-speed, high-quality printers or scanners and can be used to establish systems where customers pay for printing. They can provide a single software platform for access to electronic products, reducing the special configurations needed for individual computers. These improvements must be weighed against the potential increased cost of network licenses and the necessity to have trained staff available to maintain the system.

5. New Products and Initial Release Issues

Frequently, new products and system upgrades contain bugs that have not been detected by the producer. Software is particularly prone to this syndrome; therefore, not all upgrades are necessarily a good thing. Caution is prudent when deciding whether to implement a new product as there may be unintended results, especially with Web browsers and system software. In addition, what might look like new enhancements could pose problems for less experienced users who are accustomed to using older, simpler products. In some situations a library may find itself buying a second release of an item to correct shortcomings in the first release. Product reviews are common in the appropriate literature, and these can help identify bugs and shortcomings of a new offering. Delaying purchase of an item in electronic format until professional reviewers have assessed it is a prudent course. Also, systems staff need to be involved with new software and upgrades to test and review them in a safe environment—before they are installed system wide.

Systems staff, library staff, and library patrons should be involved in the review process for electronic resources. New acquisitions in this area must have a high rate of patron acceptance in the short term to be considered cost effective, and products and upgrades need to work as intended. Electronic products are generally very expensive. Since the costs are high, administrators want to see use statistics that will justify the expense. If patrons don't accept and use a product, the continued purchase of the product should be questioned. A number of ways are available to involve users in the review process. Most products offer limited trials prior to purchase. Before a library acquires trial access or a review copy, it should read carefully all agreements that govern the trial use. In some instances, signing a license will be necessary. For an item that comes on physical media (software, CD, etc.), the library may need to assent to an agreement governing its return and may also be liable for the full cost of the item if not returned within a specified amount of time. The library should encourage staff and patrons to use the test product. It is useful to set up a link in the online catalog or library website to the trial product and establish an easy way for users to provide feedback. This allows staff and patrons to work with an item in different environments and establishes a clear source of feedback for selectors. If the library can identify remote users who are willing to test a product, it should contact them and ask them to review the product. This will provide information on how the product functions in a remote-access environment.

Another way that staff and users can obtain helpful information about a product is through electronic bulletin boards and online user groups. By communicating with such groups, staff and users can discuss a product with other individuals who have used it and do not necessarily have an interest in selling the item. User groups are also invaluable in detecting bugs in upgrades that publishers have missed.

A further option for previewing a potential acquisition is to volunteer the library as a beta test site. The beta test of a product is the final stage in the testing of a product before its commercial release. By participating in a product test and giving feedback, librarians may have some impact on the product's final design. Sometimes vendors and publishers also offer significant discounts to beta test participants. They benefit by getting the reactions of consumers to their products prior to full release and can make improvements based on ideas generated by the beta test.

C. Other Considerations

1. Local Participation and Assessment of User Needs

Competition for scarce resources is not new to the library world. Accountability is becoming a major concern in today's decision-making activities. Therefore, it is imperative for a library to have a clear understanding of the needs of its users. Such an understanding gives a library's selectors a better chance of obtaining support for their decisions. The assessment of user needs is a determining factor in collection development endeavors and in selection activities. Involving users and library staff in evaluating resources identified for potential acquisition is crucial. They can provide invaluable information regarding the usefulness of a product, evaluation of its content from their own perspective, and helping to answer such questions as "Would this product be used?" and "Does it respond to a strategic priority identified by the parent institution?"

An ongoing activity for selectors should be assessment of needs in their areas of responsibility. A library may want to consider developing an institutional approach to systematic needs assessment for the population it serves. The library can do this at intervals, surveying a portion of users at a time. A formalized approach such as this provides an expansive picture of user needs and of the demand for electronic materials as well as potential needs in the future. The focus group assessment technique gives similar results but has the added benefit of obtaining the expected return rate; in other words, knowing how many people were included in the survey and how many provided feedback.

Less formal methods for identifying user needs exist. For example, the interaction that occurs during a reference interview and subsequent assistance to the user provides an inquisitive librarian with valuable information about needs. Informal conversations or interviews with faculty and graduate students are also opportunities to gather data in a less structured setting. Information that a library needs to collect includes current programmatic needs, emerging areas of study, user groups who will benefit the most by adding certain types of resources in certain electronic media, and the level of information required by those groups.

Given the abundance of options currently available, selectors need to be more cautious than ever. Additional mechanisms for involving users in the selection process can be incorporated in various ways. For example, if preview copies are available, acquire these and give staff and users an opportunity to use them before purchasing.

a. Before accepting a review copy, carefully read all agreements that govern its use.

b. Encourage staff and patrons to try out the review or trial version.

c. Establish a clear communication mechanism between the users trying the product and the selector(s) involved in the process, allowing the opportunity to provide feedback.

2. Standards

Standards allow libraries to fulfill their mission to provide access to information and to share resources. Their use permits libraries to communicate with each other using a "common language."

Libraries should carefully assess a publisher's compliance with national standards and the intended local use of particular products before purchasing them. Although standardization has come a long way in the last few years, particularly with the incorporation of the Z39.50 standard, not all aspects of electronic publishing are covered by American National Standards Institute (ANSI) or International Standards Organization (ISO) standards. The Z39.50 standard allows an application on one computer to query a database on another. Software executing a "title" search in one database can, using Z39.50, execute the same "title" search in another database

As the electronic publishing industry continues to evolve and grow at a fast pace, some products become available before standards governing them are in place. Selectors and others involved in the selection process should determine which standards are applicable to their use of the product and then determine if the publisher is meeting the standards. Of particular concern is the application of standards related to the content of electronic versions of products (such as a serial) versus the content of the printed version.

The ISO archiving standards for interoperability of digital archives currently under development will address a widespread concern shared by preservation librarians and archivists concerning the archiving of electronic information (see http://ssdoo.gsfc.nasa.gov/nost/isoas/). In particular, the need to regularly refresh (update) information stored in electronic formats must be addressed so that they will not become outdated as storage media change. The application of the interoperability standard will make possible the transfer of archives from one electronic format to a newer, more powerful and reliable one.

Standards affecting an institution's ability to fully participate in interlibrary loan operations should also influence selection decisions. Luckily, the National Information Standards Organization (NISO) has provided ample information that's widely accessible on its website (http://www.niso.org) regarding standards that apply to the information industry and their current status of development or implementation.

3. Preservation

An institution's selection and purchase of electronic materials must take into account preservation issues associated with its future ability to provide "perpetual" access to the digital materials it owns. It is particularly important to address the preservation of electronic materials, since the medium does not offer the long-term life expectancy or the stability of more traditional media, such as paper or microform. Many libraries are offering wide electronic access to resources without ensuring the future availability of these resources.

Preservation is an issue that libraries need to clearly establish in their collection development policies. Such a policy should determine the level of commitment an institution is willing to make. Unfortunately, it must not only be based on commitment or belief but also an estimation of the resources available for investment coupled with an awareness of uncertainties about the technology in the future.

Preservation efforts for digital materials should include resources originally published in digital format (such as electronic journals or websites) and should not be limited to those published in traditional formats, such as paper or microform, and then digitized. An institution must consider the future availability of all types of formats when approaching this issue. The endeavor will require a commitment of staff, funds, and, most importantly, long-term support from the institution's top administrators. The Digital Millennium Copyright Act (DMCA) and other legal initiatives, such as the Uniform Computer Information Transactions Act (UCITA), could present major legal problems (see chapter V, section G.2 for discussion of these issues).

Many efforts are under way to establish archives. Some consortia are creating "last copy collections," which are storehouses for paper copies of electronic products. This type of collection ensures the existence of a permanent archive and allows individual consortium members to shift exclusively to electronic access with assurance that the information will be archived. In other projects, libraries or consortia are storing their electronic data and in this way guaranteeing permanent electronic access for their members. In some situations, publishers have based their business models on a commitment to provide continuing access. However, any third party, including OCLC, a publisher, or a consortium, can have financial difficulties and limit or cease operations. Individual institutions must decide for themselves the amount of risk they are willing to accept.

The preservation issue is very complex and is currently receiving significant attention within the library profession. Although a full review of current arguments does not fall within the parameters of this book, it is important to mention some of the major points of debate and concern.

a. Migration of information from one digital medium to another, also referred as "refreshing," consists of transferring digital information contained in one electronic medium into another, such as from a CD-ROM to the Internet.

b. The costs involved in refreshing digital data is an area of concern.

c. Different media have different life spans. For example, the life span of an archival microform could be as long as five hundred years, but that of magnetic media is between five and ten years, if that.

d. Technological obsolescence happens very quickly due to ongoing changes in technology used to access and service electronic materials. The hardware and software in use today will not likely be operational with tomorrow's resources.

e. The "emulation" technique has been developed as a digital preservation strategy. For example, a library would keep data in its original format and would force new systems to emulate the old ones in order to maintain the usability of the data.

f. An important issue is the lack of sufficient standards, especially those relevant to metadata description. Metadata are structured data that describe a resource's attributes, characterize its relationships, and support its discovery, management, and effective use in an electronic environment.

g. Criteria need to be established to describe what digital resources should be preserved and how.

IV

Acquisitions

The acquisition of electronic information is a process that is both relatively new and very important for libraries. It is an area that is seeing significant growth and, since it is new, still presents considerable challenges. Many elements of the process are similar to those of the print acquisitions process, but even more are very different. Traditional boundaries between technical services, collection development and management, systems, and public services become blurred and indistinct when dealing with electronic information acquisitions. Each of these areas must make decisions affecting how an electronic resource is purchased.

A. Major Issues to Be Considered during the Acquisition Process

1. Purchase Agreements

One of the most important decisions involved in the purchase of electronic information products pertains to the issue of access. Often, information in electronic format is leased, not sold. For a fee, a publisher will allow a subscriber to use its product for a specified period of time and in specific ways. If a subscription is not renewed, access to the product ends. Since some publishers offer either leased access or ownership rights to the same product in license agreements, a library will need to determine which arrangement best suits its needs. It is always a good idea to negotiate perpetual rights for electronic products, either through Web access or electronic copy. Outright purchase is frequently more expensive than a short-term lease, but it bestows much more value. When a lease purchase agreement ends, all data are returned to the publisher or destroyed, meaning that there is no continuing value for the dollars invested. With ownership, however, an institution can expect to have indefinite access to the purchased data, one way or another. Ownership is not always an option. Sometimes publishers will not grant continuing rights. Some publishers do not want to lose control of their revenue, and they believe that by working with a lease model they can maintain their revenues. Also, publishers often do not sell full-text providers the rights to the content they include in their databases. Consequently the providers cannot offer ownership-purchasing models to their licensees.

Before ordering electronic products, be sure that all terms of the purchase arrangements are clear—especially those regarding ownership or access. All required changes to the terms should be negotiated with the publisher before purchasing. This negotiation is a customary part of the licensing process. Publishers are often willing to modify agreements if a library requires the changes before purchasing an item. Negotiating with a publisher of electronic information is never unproductive even if it does not result in changes in the agreement. The process makes the publisher more aware of the needs of libraries and possibly more attuned to the library market in the future. If compliance with an agreement is difficult or impossible and the publisher will not change the terms, refrain from purchasing the item. If an item is purchased through a vendor or supplier, remember that the vendor is a second party and its interpretation of a lease may not be binding. Often publishers do not offer uniform agreements for all their products. Careful reading of agreements is strongly recommended. Items to consider include the following:

a. The agreement or license should clearly delineate the terms of ownership or lease. These should include a description of the length of the agreement (including start and stop dates), a description of the entire product including (if applicable) which backfiles are being acquired, the ownership of these backfiles, how often updates are to be received, and the disposition of superseded files.

b. The agreement should clearly indicate all usage or copyright restrictions. The intended use of a product within an organization may be severely restricted by rights reserved by the publisher. Do not assume that a specific use is allowed if not clearly stated in the purchase agreement. If a specific use is required, it's best to have it in writing.

c. If hardware is to be included, the agreement should state whether the equipment is leased or purchased and should address the maintenance responsibility. If the seller provides maintenance, the terms of service should be defined (for example, the computer will be repaired or replaced in twenty-four hours).

d. Product warranties need to be clearly stated in the agreement and understood by the library.

The juxtaposition of access and ownership has been precipitated by the huge increase in information available in electronic form and a proliferation of systems used to supply the information. Electronic products offer access to a wide variety of resources that are not always owned by the library. Traditionally, interlibrary loan services satisfied patrons' demands for material not available in the local library. Now, information not available locally can be obtained in a number of ways, either in print or electronically. Some of the new electronic information sources can provide either a full or truncated version of text on a remote server. A library may identify information resources online and purchase them from external suppliers on an as-needed basis. In other cases, the library may not even "own" the electronic products, but rather lease or share them in a consortium. One of the decision points to be considered when purchasing electronic information products involves the question of whether the item should be subscribed to through a license or accessed online on a "pay-per-use" basis. Pay-per-use is also referred to as "pay-per-view," "pay-per-search," and "pay-by-the-drink." It is important to keep in mind that, as technology and the ways of providing of information products advance, products or services chosen today may be obsolete tomorrow.

Some vendors are aggressively marketing online access to remote databases through the use of Web-based "user-friendly" gateways. The development of standards for sharing electronic information, such as Z39.50, a NISO communication protocol, or the Bath Profile, will make gateway use more common. The Bath Profile is an international Z39.50 specification supporting library applications and facilitates searching across multiple systems. The Association of Research Libraries Scholars Portal project also will extend Web-based access across multiple platforms. These developments could make investment in the local or regional ownership of large information products mounted in a local computer system a difficult financial decision, especially when the total cost of local hardware, storage, and maintenance is considered. With enhanced searching capabilities that link multiple sources and the added expense of maintaining local files, local access loses some of its attraction. On the other hand, hardware and software purchased locally could also be used to support future ventures in electronic publishing, as digitizing and publishing local information becomes more commonplace.

A library should weigh the current and anticipated needs of its users against its resources when making the decision to purchase electronic resources and determining how to provide access to them. Some issues the library should consider when developing its ownership/access formula are:

a. the percentage of the materials budget that should be allocated to the acquisition of traditional print and nonprint materials, ownership of electronic information products, and access to outside electronic resources

b. the sources of revenue for online document delivery services

c. staff training in the efficient use of new electronic resources

d. availability of backfiles through a one-time purchase rather than as part of a continuing annual fee arrangement (Usually the one-time purchase is cheaper, but the cost of the backfiles purchase must be carefully considered in light of the cost of providing the current data.)

e. legal issues governing the local use of electronic products, such as copyright restrictions on downloading information from databases and license limitations on product access

2. Documentation

The manuals, thesauri, and other documentation supplied with an electronic information product are important. Electronic texts, which are simply manuscripts in a digitized format, may require very simple explanations before use. On the other hand, large data sets that use special software for information organization and retrieval could require extensive use of manuals and thesauri to be successfully operated. The quality of information provided to instruct the user in the operation of a product can either enhance the usefulness of a system or greatly detract from it. The documentation need not be in printed form. Many systems offer high-quality online instructions and help as integral parts of their packages. A good source of detailed information about the documentation of a product can be found in product reviews or the publisher's documentation. Often additional software guides and manuals are available separately from those that come with the product. These independently prepared guides are usually written after a product's release and are widely available in software stores.

The usefulness of publishers' documentation is in direct relation to the computer literacy level of staff and users. A very knowledgeable staff and clientele will require fewer training guides and will make the need for high-level documentation less of a concern. However, poor documentation can greatly reduce the overall acceptance and effectiveness of information in electronic format. In fact, the "friendliness" of the documentation may influence the actual physical location of the electronic source in relation to the location of personal assistance in the library.

3. Warranties

There is a wide variance in warranties provided for electronic formats and the hardware that supports them. Some products are fully warranted against theft or damage; others carry no warranty at all and must be replaced at full cost if problems arise. Warranty is normally addressed in the license agreement. Publishers commonly attempt to disclaim responsibility for the accuracy of their product and will not warrant delivery in light of the normal vagaries of the Web. Some hardware comes with full maintenance included in its cost; others come with no maintenance or warranty at all. For CD-ROMs and other video-based media, the warranty is a real concern as the cost of replacing lost or damaged discs or tapes could become a significant factor if not planned for in advance. CD-ROMs are not indestructible as was first believed and replacement charges can have a very serious impact on the overall cost of a title.

Publishers sometimes allow subscribers to make backup copies of their products or to perform multiple "installations" of the software from a set of discs. However, some publishers tightly control the ability of the software to be copied. Consequently, an institution may need to purchase an additional copy if it requires more than the allowed number of backup copies. The DMCA limits the extent to which a library can duplicate a copyrighted product unless the product has specific protocols for creating copies.

For other types of media, such as CD-ROMs and videotapes, warranty and replacement policies vary from full replacement of lost, stolen, or damaged items to a very restrictive policy in which the user is fully responsible for replacing lost or damaged items—in other words, no warranty at all. Current technology makes full-scale copying of many CD-ROMs and videodiscs nearly impossible. Even in cases where copying of a CD-ROM product is possible, copyright and license restrictions would likely forbid full-scale copying. The library, therefore, may be completely dependent on the publisher for replacement of such products if they are lost, stolen, or damaged.

4. Copyright

The field of electronic publishing is changing rapidly and how current copyright laws will have an impact on it is not absolutely clear. Due to the lack of clarity in the applications of the fair use doctrine to electronic information, most licenses seek to define rights and privileges and to establish what defines "fair use" of the product. At the time of this writing, if not specifically addressed in the license, the fair use doctrine applies in the same way to information in electronic format as it applies to printed materials. Some people contend that fair use allows downloading or copying of information for educational and research purposes. Established guidelines for print materials define the percentage of a printed work that may be copied for educational purposes. However, what constitutes fair use of information in electronic format is not clear. To complicate matters, many producers of software and commercial electronic media are attempting to remove most of the protections from current laws that libraries have enjoyed in the past. Legislative efforts are under way to completely change what constitutes the fair use of electronic information, including the Uniform Computer Information Transactions Act (UCITA) (see chapter V, section G. 2 for discussion of these issues). The DMCA also has a chilling effect on copyright issues pertaining to the fair use of electronic information. For the time being, the safest course is to negotiate allowances for required uses of a product into the license.

For most purposes, libraries already limit the use of electronic information in ways that generally maintain compliance with fair use guidelines. For example, because of high demand for computer terminals, most use is limited to intervals of time that are too short to allow users an opportunity to copy or download amounts of information that could be questioned under fair use guidelines. However, as local systems increase in speed and capacity for downloading, libraries in educational settings may need to post online notices to inform their users about the fair use limitations on the information available in the system. Educating patrons about what generally is accepted as fair use is important. Notices on a library's local system certainly will not stop a determined information abuser but can reduce its liability and prevent unintentional copyright violations. Education is critical, as some users believe that everything they find on the Web, even copyrighted materials, is free for their use and can be included on personal Web pages or in other public applications. Such users must learn what constitutes fair use in this new environment. Many license agreements mandate user notification about copyright limitations.

In most situations, publishers of electronic formats define what they consider to be fair use of their product in their license agreements if they are concerned that general copyright limitations do not protect their product. Some publishers incorporate technologies into their systems that make it virtually impossible to download extremely large portions of data. Others monitor the use of their products and report and investigate unusually heavy activity. The issue of copyright for electronic formats is one that will remain unclear for most libraries until it is addressed in legislation. Unfortunately, most legislative initiatives to date have not been beneficial for consumers and instead protect the commercial rights of publishers. If this trend continues, it may be necessary to reintroduce fair use through the licensing process.

Those responsible for license compliance in libraries need to make sure that all license agreements with publishers are enforced. Software should not be available to more than one user at a time unless the license specifically allows it. If a compliance issue is unclear and in dispute, great caution must be exercised before committing to a course of action.

B. Mechanics of the Order Process

Materials in electronic formats can be published as either monographs or serials, although these terms begin to break down in the electronic environment. The actual mechanics of the order process for electronic formats differ little from standard methods established for books and serials at one level but present a whole new set of challenges at another level. As with their printed counterparts, the ways that electronic serials and monographs are processed are distinctly different. This guide describes only the most basic elements. Refer to the American Library Association's ALCTS Acquisition Guides series for supplementary information on ordering materials. More information about the Guides series is available at www.alastore.ala.org.

Generally speaking, the same procedures apply to the purchase of an electronic product as those applied to the purchase of any other type of item. Libraries need to establish a clear "paper trail" that describes what is purchased from which source. Purchases of licenses are heavily involved and the purchase order is sometimes supplanted by the license agreement. In such cases, it is still a good idea to document the purchase with purchase orders in local systems and to keep payment records. One major difference between purchasing print materials and electronic resources is the ability of local online systems to provide value-added services that support the order function. Many local systems do an adequate job of tracking orders, claiming and checking continuing orders, and providing routines for claiming orders or subscriptions that do not arrive. Similar value-added functions for electronic purchasing have not yet become common parts of most library systems. Some data elements that should be used to help manage the purchase of electronic products are not available in most local systems. Although the development of local tracking systems to manage the electronic product acquisitions process is becoming quite common, at this time no best practice has emerged.

1. Standard Order Form Information

Whether a library mails, faxes, or sends purchase orders online, it should supply clearly labeled information. This information includes the following bibliographic product details for electronic formats:

a. title, authorship, or statement of responsibility
b. edition statement
c. publishing information or imprint
d. any specific number associated with the item being ordered, such as ISBN, ISSN, bar code/product code, vendor, or publisher inventory numbers
e. purchase order number
f. order date
g. number of copies requested
h. variant ship-to and bill-to locations
i. estimated price
j. vendor information
k. tax-exempt identifier

Additional information for continuing orders (including serials):

a. volume numbering
b. coverage of backfiles ordered

c. frequency of new issues

d. starting volume and corresponding date

e. length of subscription (one year, two years, etc.)

In some automated purchasing systems, data codes can be established to record the specific format of the material ordered. This can be an important management tool for a library. One drawback, however, is that with each new product format that is introduced, a new code must be added to the ordering system. Additionally, the system may be able to store other important information, such as special handling-on-arrival instructions, requestor name, or library location. If special fields are not available for these items (especially requestor), the acquisitions system may be able to record this information as internal notes. Of course, the library fund and estimated price must be stored in the library system so that funds are properly encumbered and later expended for the purchase.

2. Special Order Form Instructions and Information

The foregoing purchase order information generally parallels that used for most book and serial purchases in print format. Expediting the fulfillment of orders for materials in electronic format requires the inclusion of special types of information:

a. type of access (Web access, etc.)

b. institutional IP addresses, including proxy servers

c. name, address, phone and fax numbers, and e-mail address for the local technical contact

d. product version

e. expected start date

f. number of simultaneous users (if applicable)

g. bill-to and ship-to addresses, as well as addresses for the technical contact and for a contact for licensing issues

h. exact type of computer for software (for example, IBM or Apple)

i. complete description of the package being ordered if purchasing bundled hardware and software, including:

- RAM capacity
- CD-ROM, DVD, hard and floppy drives, and disk sizes that can be accommodated
- monitor
- software to be included (Windows, etc.)
- keyboard style, mouse, etc.

It may be useful to separate the backfile order from the continuing order for the same product. The backfile would represent a one-time purchase, while the continuing order would be a serial order. For example, a library is generating an order for the serial title *xyz*. The journal charges $150 per year for an ongoing subscription. However, they charge a $50 one-time fee for access to the previous five years of the publication or a $250 one-time fee for access to the entire set of backfiles. The backfile could be handled as a one-time order and the continuation as a serial order. The anticipated future cost of the product would be based on payments for the serial record; the expenditure for the backfile should not be used in cost projections.

Purchase orders should be sent out on a regular basis to maintain processing efficiency at both ends of the transactions. Vendors and publishers of electronic products often deal only in the electronic medium and their order volume is much less than that of a major book or serial publisher. Consequently, a library can expect a faster rate of order fulfillment, with turnaround occurring anywhere between four and eight weeks. However, if a license is involved, fulfillment time is determined more by the licensing process than by the order process. In fact, in such cases, the purchase order is a formality; the signing of the license is considered the point of purchase. If an item is needed in a short time frame, the library can expedite the process by communicating directly with the publisher and making efforts to complete the licensing process as quickly as possible. Again, licensing will slow things down. For print material, some publishers accept orders over the telephone with a purchase order number and ship the order with a "pro forma" invoice. Also, rush procedures can be worked out in advance with vendors. Because of the complexities of licensing, the ability to quickly obtain access is far less common. Fewer publishers are willing to set up access without a fully executed license in place. If such is the case and time is an issue, explore setting up trial access.

3. Receipt and Payment Arrangements

A library may want to separate funds for materials in electronic formats in order to track expenditures for budget planning and allocation review purposes in these emerging areas. In many situations, the start-up costs are much more significant than those for periodic updates. Also, the initial start-up costs increase greatly when substantial backfiles are purchased. Consequently, the first year's charges cannot be used to indicate future costs, and expenditure reports may not be a good predictor for the next year's budget.

The procedures associated with the receipt and payment for items in electronic format is very similar to those for books and serials. Access to the purchased product needs to be verified. This can be a major stumbling block since so many twists and turns occur in the licensing, purchasing, and payment processes. It is sometimes hard to tell when a transaction is complete and payment should be made. In the case of physical items, a library needs to carefully compare the physical item received with the order to ensure that what was received is what was ordered. For CD-ROMs, individuals receiving materials should not break the shrink wrap until someone has reviewed the packaging for a license (see chapter V, Licensing). The validity of shrink-wrap licenses is in dispute, but caution could save costly litigation. For electronic-only products, some procedure needs to be established that allows for the review of items in process and to verify electronic access as part of the payment (or similar) process.

Depending on the return privileges granted by a vendor, a library may want to delay payment for a product until it reviews the material for defects. Damage to printed materials is fairly obvious but detecting damage or defects in electronic information requires closer inspection and use.

Publishers or vendors may require prepayment before online access is activated or the product shipped. Such a practice has potential to cause problems for buyers if access is not turned on or if the material is either not shipped promptly or not shipped at all. Local automated systems will not be able to help staff by alerting them that access has not been established. With print products, claims are automatically generated for items not received. But for their electronic counterparts, there is no physical item to receive and no process within the local system to alert staff to "no access." The creation of stand-alone licensing and electronic resources management systems is becoming more common in response to these issues. For more about these developments, see www.library.cornell.edu/cts/elicensestudy/ and section 9 on management systems below. Libraries should stay informed about potential problems with certain companies and never ship substantial prepayments to post office boxes or organizations with which they are unfamiliar.

4. Claims

As currency of coverage is quite important for most electronic products, establishing a separate claim cycle for these items may be necessary. Local library systems work well in generating claims for orders of physical items, such as CD-ROMs, videos, and software on discs. A unique process for electronic products could be established to generate claims in a relatively short period of time. Local systems will not work well for purchasing electronic products that are access only. Libraries may need to develop electronic resource and licensing "databases" to track such products. These databases issue "ticklers" to initiate reviews for items in the licensing process or awaiting online start-up. Depending on the volume of electronic product purchases, the database can be a simple paper file or a complex online system. If an institution purchases only four or five electronic products each year, a simple paper system may work. For organizations that purchase thousands of electronic products annually, online systems will be needed.

If an order remains unfilled after a long period of time, it is prudent to check with the publisher for the availability of newer versions of the product. The shelf life of electronic products is short, and if the product has been updated, the most current version is normally desired.

Determining why purchased access has not been turned on will become libraries' claiming challenge of the future as the industry shifts from paper publishing to electronic-only publishing. Activity will swing from claiming missing books and journals to resolving access problems with electronic products. The regular processing of claims for print materials will gradually decrease as fewer print items are purchased, but new processes will emerge that engage staff in troubleshooting access for electronic products. Staff will also face potential problems when electronic-only Web access is established for journals, but new issues are not posted in a timely manner. This kind of claim activity is usually an ad hoc process and generally is initiated when a user notices that a new journal issue is not available. Considering the investment in electronic journals, this will be an area to watch.

5. Cancellations and Returns

An electronic information product license should specifically define the terms for cancellation. If it does not, procedures and routines should be established for canceling orders with the vendor or publisher. Even if the license does define the cancellation terms, there are internal procedures that the library should follow to correctly update records, some of which are listed as follows:

a. When canceling a product, a library should update the internal records to indicate when the item is canceled, who canceled it, and when the cancellation is effective.

b. The library should place a note in the record describing how and when the cancellation was forwarded to the producer.

c. The library should establish with the publisher an agreed-on time period beyond which it will consider the order canceled if still unfulfilled.

d. A claim period can be programmed into many automated acquisitions systems to generate claims on a regular basis for unfulfilled orders and, after "x" number of claims, an alert is issued for follow-up action.

e. A library may choose to cancel an outstanding order after the initial claim period expires for various reasons:

- variables such as the likelihood that the item will never be received, the priority of the item, the number of alternative sources for the item or for similar titles, and the impact on the current budget

- concerns about the cost per use for electronic products that are very expensive and/or infrequently used
- freeing encumbered funds through the regular cancellation of unfulfilled orders and minimizing the number of outstanding orders that can complicate the closing of the budget at the end of the budget year

f. Cancellations sometimes involve titles that are received on a continuing basis; in such cases, the process will be similar to canceling print serials.

- If a library is canceling an order in which it has purchased continuing rights to data, it should make arrangements for transfer of the data to local systems or for ongoing online access.
- The library should check the license to determine if it specifies a timetable for cancellation; for example, ninety days before the renewal date.
- The library should take into account the frequency of the publication when establishing the cancellation date.

g. A library may be able to obtain a refund or credit for a cancellation made before the end of the subscription period, but it will need to negotiate this with the publisher or vendor.

h. After cancellation, some publishers require the return of leased or licensed electronic products and associated materials, such as disks or tapes. They may also require the removal of all copies of the products from local systems.

i. When shifting a product order from both paper and electronic formats to an electronic-only format, a library needs to carefully update the records to clearly document the transition. Records for paper resources need to indicate when the subscription ends and when access will truly become electronic only.

j. Libraries will have to return items from time to time for a number of reasons, including:

- duplicate receipts—two or more copies of the ordered item are received
- receipt of incorrect materials from the publisher
- defective copies
- publisher requirements to return older versions of materials (e.g., superseded CD-ROMs) whenever newer versions are to be distributed

A library should take care to communicate precisely why it is returning an item and, if returning it on account of shortcomings, the nature of a complaint. It should update its local records with information concerning what was returned and when. The majority of publishers and vendors are reasonable when confronted with returned products, but some may take issue. The library should be selective when choosing a product source. Cheap mail-order houses and cut-rate hardware producers may appear inexpensive on the surface but often prove expensive in the end, as they do not provide a level of customer service that makes problem resolution easy.

6. Review Copies and Product Trials

Information in electronic format is often the most expensive material that libraries buy. It is common practice in some sectors of the industry to ship items on approval or as review copies. Sometimes the review copy is a sample of the product that presents the basic system and a few test records. This kind of review copy is easy to deal with, as it is either very inexpensive to purchase or is sent gratis and is disposable. In other situations, the review copy is not so easy to handle, in particular when the review copy is the actual product and is accompanied by a notice of a specific return date or it will be considered purchased. In many cases, the notice becomes an invoice after the review period expires. A library should avoid accepting a review copy in this manner if the length of the review period is potentially not manageable; if so, it may want to negotiate a longer review period before or immediately after receipt.

As the Web continues to develop as the delivery mechanism of choice for electronic products, the use of review copies to evaluate items continues to decline in favor of online trials. Trials are fairly easy to set up, but in some situations the publisher will require the library to sign a license beforehand. Publishers that require a license are not trying to obstruct the process but simply want to protect their product. For online trials the licensing process is normally much simpler than for purchasing, since many of the contentious issues, such as rights for interlibrary loan and use in electronic reserves, are moot in trials. Though the negotiation process and the terms may be simpler, the license is still a real license and will need to be signed by an authorized person and enforced like any other license.

When setting up trials, libraries should, if possible, link the trial to the online catalog or home page. The product should be clearly labeled as a trial, a link for feedback easily available, and the time frame for the trial clearly outlined. Because patron expectations are sometimes difficult to manage, it is advisable to include a disclaimer indicating that the trial version does not imply that the full version of the product will soon be purchased.

7. Pricing

The price structures used to market electronic information are complex and much more challenging to unravel than the pricing systems of printed materials. A product's price can vary according to the size and type of the organization purchasing it, the expected number of simultaneous users, overlap of the product with similar products already purchased, the total expected use, and just about any other variable a publisher wishes to use. When in doubt, a library should ask for a quote and not be afraid to offer to pay less. Discounts are not standardized due to the wide variety of publishers, vendors, and products. Publishers and vendors sometimes offer discounted prices (based on the full retail cost, sometimes difficult to determine) for the purchase of multiple copies or several expensive purchases. This is a common way library consortia work with publishers to reduce costs for participants (see chapter VI, Consortial Purchasing). There are several basic pricing models:

a. Subscription-based. Pricing is based on an annual subscription cost. For many subscription packages, publishers will base their offer on current prices for print subscriptions in an effort to protect their revenue streams and ensure that income does not drop while shifting from print to electronic products.

- Electronic-only subscriptions. Many publishers will reduce pricing for libraries that switch to electronic-only ("e-only") products. E-only products do reduce some publishing costs, especially those associated with printing and shipping. Large reductions are not fully feasible at this time since most publishers must maintain the infrastructure for delivering both print products and electronic content and end up splitting business between the two models. However, libraries can certainly save dollars by shifting from paper or paper-plus-electronic orders to e-only orders. Keep in mind that e-only orders may involve risk until the issues relating to permanent archiving of electronic products have been resolved.
- Electronic-plus-paper subscriptions, including deep discount pricing. This pricing model remains popular because archival access to the owned data is guaranteed. Paper copies are still received and archived locally. Some extra costs are associated with paper-plus-electronic packages. Generally speaking, there is a basic subscription cost and then additional charges for the "extra." If a resource is priced according to the paper subscription costs, then the extra is a surcharge for electronic access. If the basic subscription is for the content in electronic format, then the extra is a charge for paper copies. This pricing method is often referred to as the deep discount price (DDP). Generally, the electronic-only or content pricing is 85 percent to 95 percent of the normal paper subscription costs. The DDP ranges from 10 percent to 40 percent of the paper subscription cost. Great variation exists among these pricing models and the numbers here are included only as very general guides.

- Additional pricing models. In other subscription models, additional journals in electronic format (not paper) may be included in the package as an enticement to protect the publisher's overall bottom line. These types of packages are most frequently seen in consortial purchases, whereby titles subscribed to by one member of the consortium are made available electronically to all other members at little or no added cost. To safeguard its income, the publisher often attempts to extend the length of the contract and place restrictions on cancellations, offsetting the benefits of the additional access. A variation of this model is the whole-package model, the proverbial "big deal." In this model, nearly all of the publisher's products are available electronically in the package as long as subscriptions are maintained to those titles that are subscribed to currently. Opinions of the value of these packages differ widely. Some view them as effective means of expanding access to information. Others view them as tools that publishers use to lock customers into purchasing their products and artificially protect their marginal journals from market forces potentially forcing the journals' demise. Before signing on to "big deals," a library should carefully review the pros and cons and the long-term consequences.

   b. Access-based pricing models. Some publishers price their products according to the number of simultaneous users or ports purchased. The publisher limits the use of its product to x number of users at one time. This can be advantageous as a library can purchase as much access as is required, and reduced access is frequently cheaper than unlimited access. A drawback is that users are turned away if all ports are currently in use. Usage reports need to be monitored to ensure that access purchased does match user needs. If the number of users denied access is high, then it may be necessary to purchase access for more simultaneous users. If the number is small, the level of access purchased may be too great; some savings could be achieved by reducing the number of simultaneous users allowed.

   c. Site license–based pricing models. These pricing models are the flip side of the access-based models, offering unlimited access to a product no matter how many people might be using it at the same time. Site licenses can be cost effective if use is expected to be high. For access-based models, the more access a library purchases, the lower the cost per user. In the upper parts of the range, the pricing is not very different from site-license pricing. If a library expects a product to have high usage, then this pricing model is a good choice. Some site-license price structures have a fixed price; others vary based on such criteria as the size of the potential user population.

   d. "Pay-per-use" access. In some cases, full-text products are made available on a pay-as-you-go basis, whereby the publishers charge for only what is used. This pricing model is not widely available due to the high cost of the infrastructure needed to keep track of billing and information delivery in this environment. Many use studies indicate that the cost per use of some electronic products is consistently high across different institutions. When a library needs to offer access to an expensive product but expects usage to be low, it may benefit from this model.

e. Subscription supplemented by "pay-per-use." This model combines subscription for a core collection of materials with a supplemental pay-per-use arrangement for other content. This combines good aspects of both models. The high-use content that would be prohibitively expensive on a pay-per-use basis can be acquired by subscription, while those areas for which subscriptions would not be cost effective can be acquired on a pay-per-use basis. A library can purchase access to an entire content package at an affordable price.

These pricing models are not available for all products or from all publishers. Some publishers may offer only a single pricing model for their products without any choices. Some products offer only slight variations in pricing models at best. The electronic publishing industry is changing rapidly, and the pricing structures are shifting accordingly. Within a short period of time, the models mentioned previously will likely be supplanted by others. When negotiating prices, a library should not be afraid to explore different models, even if not offered—it will not hurt to ask. Also, the library should not be reluctant to move completely away from the standard pricing models and simply offer a bottom-line price. Another approach is to offer a specific dollar amount and ask what the publisher can offer for it. Also, when negotiating prices, the library should not assume that a quote made several weeks ago is still current today.

8. The Role of Vendors

Materials in electronic format are frequently acquired directly from the publisher because the publisher is the sole source for the items. Publishers sometimes offer discounts based on volume or other considerations, such as concurrent ownership of the title in paper or other formats. Prepublishing discounts that are available for purchasing the item prior to the actual publication can sometimes reduce cost. Negotiating directly with publishers is the best way to obtain discounts, and the most cost-effective way is to negotiate with publishers through a consortium. Some publishers offer their best prices to consortia of users. For further information on consortial purchasing, see chapter VI, Consortial Purchasing.

In some situations it may not be practical to purchase directly from a publisher. Vendors are still very important to the purchasing process, especially for serial subscriptions. Subscription agents bring many value-added features to the business relationship that publishers as a whole do not offer. In the electronic environment, subscription agents supply libraries with electronic invoices that post to local systems with a minimum of effort. Allocating local funds at discrete levels requires detailed payment information for journal titles so that expenditures can be charted against allocations. This kind of detailed, loadable expenditure information is not available from publishers as they have not developed internal systems that can produce invoice data in formats usable in most library management systems. Vendors have invested in the development of proprietary interfaces needed to load financial data into a variety of library systems. Publishers will not do this. Vendors work with just a few systems and can distribute their costs as part of the service. Publishers sell into much more varied markets (bookstores, wholesalers, libraries, etc.) and the costs of developing interfaces for all parts of the market would be significant.

In addition, purchasing through vendors reduces the amount of checks, proof of payments, claims, etc., that libraries have to process. Publisher-specific purchasing processes, on the other hand, result in increased local processing of financial transactions, which in turn increases internal processing costs. Business relationships with vendors can reduce such internal costs. As discussed above, maintaining links and access will become the "serials claiming" of the electronic journal environment. Without electronic invoices that post detailed information in local management systems, tracking down and claiming access problems for electronic resources will be very difficult and keeping track of subscriptions and payment histories will be much more complicated. For example, when a link to an e-journal fails, proof of subscription and payment history will be difficult if detailed invoice information is not present in the local system.

Vendors also provide important pricing and collection development reports. Since they may aggregate a large part of a library's business, they can provide data and analysis that may be useful in budget allocation and collection assessment efforts. In a publisher-based purchasing model, however, this data collection and analysis must be done in-house. Staff will need to aggregate data from several disparate sources to derive good expenditure and collection management reports.

In addition, vendors act as voices for customers. When a vendor approaches a large publisher and states that it represents 30 percent of the publisher's business and that its customers are not happy, it will be heard. Even a consortium that deals extensively with a publisher will not represent as much of the publisher's business as a vendor.

Vendors do charge service fees to provide support for electronic purchases. But due to economies of scale, they can provide their services more cheaply than a library could through local processes.

Although the support for subscription-based packages that vendors provide is valuable, they are not always the most cost-effective choice. If ordering a large, expensive database, such as an A&I or a business database, it may be more cost effective to negotiate and order directly with the publisher. Before moving ahead with an acquisition, a library should review the benefits and costs of working with the vendor. In some situations the value-added services are more valuable than the service charges; in other situations they are not.

If ordering through a vendor, clarifying pricing, terms, licensing, and invoicing with the vendor and publisher will be necessary. This is especially true for e-journal packages where traditionally a subscription agent handles payment for the subscription. In the electronic environment, e-only orders may reduce the actual subscription price, but other charges may arise for e-content. A library should work through the pricing for such packages with the vendor to avoid confusion and mistaken payments. Clear communication will improve the acquisition process for both parties.

9. Management Systems for Electronic Information Resources

Most local online library management systems currently cannot provide the functionality needed to support the emerging processes that are used to manage electronic information resource acquisition. Processes for managing electronic resources are being developed that require the creation and definition of new system elements. These elements may be combined with existing data elements to form locally tailored e-resource management databases. Generally, current systems support print acquisitions well but do not provide the same level of support for electronic resources. When a patron inquires about a specific product, thinking it was ordered a long time ago, multiple queries in several areas are often required to determine what has happened. Was the item ordered? Was the license finalized? Was the invoice paid? Was access turned on? Were correct links established? Management systems need to be developed to store information that can assist with the management of electronic resources. If a library purchases few electronic products each year, an informal, manual system can effectively keep track of what is bought. The scope of electronic product acquisitions has rapidly expanded; however, its growth has outpaced the development of related tools. Several efforts are under way to create prototypes, but standards for both systems and required data elements are still being developed. Some systems that have been developed use Microsoft Access as a platform, some use Oracle, and some use other database management software. A website that offers good information on creating such systems is www.library.cornell.edu/cts/elicensestudy. Also, subscription agents and library management system vendors are likely to provide some type of management support in the future as part of their efforts to reengineer their systems for electronic resources. Several data elements are fairly common in several of the systems, including:

a. bibliographic information

- title/alternate title of the resource or e-resource package
- bibliographic record number or link to local library management system
- publisher/producer
- vendor/supplier
- electronic access provider
- format

b. licensing terms

- name of the licensed resource
- consortia involved (if any)
- license URL
- licensor, legal contact
- licensor, address information
- copyright information if held by another party
- licensee
- licensee, address information
- term/duration
- user definition
- site definition
- authentication (such as IP ranges or passwords)
- permitted uses including sharing for scholarly purposes, downloading, copying, printing, ILL-electronic or ILL-printed from electronic, inclusion in electronic reserves or course packs
- archival access/ongoing access rights
- methods for access and terms for support supplied for the product
- availability of use statistics
- confidentiality clauses
- termination/cancellation terms
- access provider
- contact/technical support and address information
- contact/sales representative and address information
- internal (library) technical support contact and address information
- internal (library) user support contact/selector and address information

c. status of the licensing process

- trial arranged/dates of trial
- status of license process—reviewed, returned to supplier, signed?
- corresponding begin/end dates
- purchase order created/item ordered? invoiced?

- access enabled
- linked

d. other information/cost data

- requestor
- selector
- package price
- list price
- purchase price
- fund line
- extra fees
- financial notes
- link to local system, order/payment systems

V

Licensing

As mentioned earlier, in today's environment most electronic resources from authoritative sources are commercially licensed for use. In nearly all cases, the licensor retains full rights to the resource; the user has only those rights designated in the license agreement. Librarians and users must remember that any licensed product is not covered by the fair use provisions of the U.S. copyright law unless specifically addressed in the license. Unfortunately copyright and fair use are not simple matters and the legal environment is built upon multiple laws and court rulings. Copyright law creates a monopoly on the subsequent use of a copyright holder's work in order to promote the creation of new knowledge and creativity for the public's benefit. This creativity is also seen as often building upon existing works, and it is this idea that is behind the fair use doctrine. This doctrine is echoed in the First Amendment's requirement of access to information as an element of free speech. Fair use is a necessary limit on that monopoly power granted under copyright laws to achieve a public good of access to and the ability to use information. Any license must be examined carefully to determine exactly which rights it grants. Whenever possible, libraries should negotiate revisions to a license to include those rights commonly granted under the fair use clause and any other terms required for reasonable local use.

Most electronic products available on physical media, such as diskette or CD-ROM, arrive shrink-wrapped with a nonnegotiable license. Some products are available at no cost but require an institution or individual end user to accept a click-on license to access them. The more expensive products that libraries acquire for patron use normally require the negotiation of a formal contract. Librarians need to be familiar with the three primary types of licenses and to establish procedures for handling them.

A. Nonnegotiable Licenses: Shrink-Wrapped and Click-On

Librarians and patrons should already be familiar with shrink-wrapped licenses as they have been packaged with software since the early 1980s. However, many have not taken the time to read and understand them. Those who have read them frequently choose to ignore their content, particularly any terms that restrict use. Users commonly assume that licensors will not find out or care about their use of a product. Librarians, however, cannot afford to take such a passive view. When a librarian acquires any licensed electronic resource on behalf of a library, she or he assumes legal and financial risks for the library and parent institution. As a safeguard, a library should consult its legal counsel to determine the legality and validity of shrink-wrapped licenses in its state. Depending on local statutes and tort law, the library may need to either recognize shrink-wrap and click-on licenses as legal contracts or safely disregard them. The Uniform Computer Information Transactions Act (UCITA) attempts to legitimize all shrink-wrapped and click-on licenses. (See section G, Other Issues, below for a more in-depth discussion of UCITA.) If either shrink-wrapped or click-on licenses are upheld to be legal, the library must treat them as any license requiring review, negotiation, and signature.

Most shrink-wrapped licenses are very difficult to edit due to the small print. Often the entire agreement, sometimes containing several paragraphs, is made so small that the entire document can fit on one side of a CD-ROM or a package of similar area. A good approach is to begin by reviewing the license and noting the terms to be changed, deleted, or added—as with any license that will be signed. Then contact the licensor and identify the person with whom to discuss these changes. This may be a complex process because shrink-wrapped licenses are so rarely altered or even questioned. Once the changes have been conveyed to the negotiating agent and the final terms are concluded, the agent usually can supply a print copy of the changes both parties have agreed to. In rare cases, the licensor will have an institutional version of the license available for negotiation. From this point on, the negotiation process is similar to that of any other signed license agreement. See appendix A for an example of a shrink-wrapped license.

Click-on licenses (see appendix B) pose similar problems because they too are not meant to be negotiated. They can often be printed from the product's website but sometimes cannot be printed as a full document due to the method in which they are provided, such as a scrolling display. They also can be difficult to locate. As with shrink-wrapped licenses, contact the licensor, identify and discuss the necessary changes, and ask for a copy of the agreed-on version of the license. Even if a click-on license is easily printed for editing, it is prudent to contact the licensor in advance and alert them to the upcoming negotiation.

If the library's legal counsel advises that shrink-wrapped or click-on licenses do not need to be reviewed, edited, and signed, its staff should still be aware of their existence. The library should review each license to identify factors that will affect the product's use. If a product's license clearly prohibits a key intended use—such as using a reasonable amount of text or data in a research paper—the library should not acquire the product without clarification from the licensor. Licensing protects both parties. Although library regulations may not obligate staff to heed shrink-wrapped or click-on licenses, they may have to negotiate terms before the product can be acquired and used effectively and legally.

Some click-on licenses are designed for the end user rather than the institution. Libraries should review such licenses in order to assure that patrons are not being asked to agree to unreasonable terms and to ensure that the terms do not subject the library to unacceptable liability. Public services staff should be aware of these licenses and be prepared to help them understand the terms and their obligation to meet them. See appendix A for a sample of a shrink-wrapped license.

B. Negotiated Licenses

Other than CD-ROM products meant to be used on single library workstations or circulated to patrons, most of a library's electronic resources will be licensed for use by the entire community. Licenses can be complex contracts requiring authorized signatures by both parties. Because licensors carry significant risk by allowing an entire community of users access to their products, product licenses may include many clauses not normally present in shrink-wrapped or click-on licenses. The acquisition process for a product should not move forward until its license is thoroughly examined, edited, negotiated, and signed by both parties. Most negotiated licenses for electronic resources are granted for specific geographical sites and clearly define access terms.

The definition of "site" varies widely among libraries, so a library will likely need to edit any site license to meet its particular needs. When a licensor defines site, it can choose from some common basic definitions: a vague general description of the physical buildings on site, a definition that focuses on a single geographical location and specifically omits additional sites, a definition that limits access to the primary administrative site, a definition based on the local area network configuration, or a definition based on the local administrative configuration. For example, a university with multiple buildings and programs distributed through a broad geographic area would likely want to define "site" according to the organizational model (one administration = one site) rather than the model that defines site as a single contiguous geographical location (many places = many sites). Site definitions are very important since the agreed-on definition has a direct impact on pricing. Some licensors attempt to use narrow site definitions in the hope of driving up charges in the future.

Licenses for most of today's electronic products also include a definition of "authorized user." A library must ensure that the definition of this term clearly encompasses the broad types of library users who will have access to the resource. Commonly, library users are defined in three basic categories: current library staff members, including permanent, temporary, contract, or visiting staff who access the system from within the library or from remote sites; individuals currently studying or using the facilities at the institution who are given access to a secure network from the library premises or such other places where the users work or study, including residence halls, offices at the institution, and homes; and any individuals who have been issued a password to use the secure system. Authorized users for corporate libraries are frequently defined as scientific, research, and support staff employed by the organization and independent contractors acting as scientific or support staff. A key issue for most site licenses is access provided to walk-in users. Either the library provides on-site authentication for guest use, or the license will have to allow all on-site use by any user.

The library can simplify the complexity of site license negotiation by preparing institutional, administrative, geographic, network, and user definitions in advance. When at the testing stage for a new product, a library can review the license for these terms and discuss them with the licensor well before the license negotiation actually begins. This type of preliminary negotiation frequently results in a revised or new version of the license and new pricing model. While the results may not be encouraging for the library, having this knowledge in advance is better than spending weeks on the testing and acquisition process only to learn that the license terms are unacceptable and the product will not be purchased after all.

C. License Review

The review of license agreements is a complex, time-consuming process and should be included in the timetable for bringing new products online. The best scenario is for a team of library staff to review each license and identify content to be edited, removed, or added. A staff member with significant licensing experience can coordinate the process and consult with other library staff to understand how the contract terms will affect the product's use. Legal counsel, or a surrogate (an individual who has been granted legal signing authority), should review and approve the license as edited by the library and should handle the final negotiations. The major difference between negotiated contracts and the nonnegotiated contracts is that the latter type of license is not intended to be reviewed.

A library should have a prepared list of essential rights that must be secured in a license; if those rights are not secured, the product should not be acquired. The library also should create a secondary list of desired, but not mandatory, rights. It can decide on a case-by-case basis whether to acquire products whose licenses do not ensure these rights even after negotiation. See appendix A for examples of what such a document might look like. Also, an example of principles that should guide the licensing process is available from the ARL at www.arl.org/scomm/licensing/principles.html. With help from legal counsel, the library should understand completely all obligations imposed by the license and be willing to meet them. If it cannot accept any of the terms in a license, it should negotiate the term so that it either becomes acceptable or is eliminated entirely. Finally, the library should prepare its own list of expectations for the licensor and ensure that the license specifies those commitments. Terms relating to local, state, and federal law should be left to legal counsel or their surrogate for review.

Once license negotiations are completed, a final agreement should be signed by both parties. The library should receive a fully executed copy of the license before it completes the acquisition process by paying the invoice. The fully executed license should be stored as part of the official legal record. Additional copies should be available for staff to consult when questions concerning the terms of the agreement arise. Exactly who signs the license agreement is a significant decision that should be made at the highest levels of the library or institution's administration. The person signing the license agreement is agreeing to the terms of a contract that legally binds the library and its parent institution. While many librarians and library administrators have the delegated authority to sign purchase agreements and issue purchase orders, the signing of a contract is not an equivalent process under the law. The right to commit funds to acquire resources is not parallel to the right to obligate an entire institution to specific legal terms with fiscal ramifications. Each institution will determine who is authorized to sign licenses based on its administrative organization. Although the authority to sign may not reside with the library staff, once the signatory is determined, the library should integrate the signing process into the overall acquisitions workload.

D. Institutional Definitions

A well-written license agreement begins with a set of definitions of terms and conditions. Before beginning the license review process, a library should create its own set of definitions for such terms as users, site, and purpose. These definitions will vary widely depending on the type of library. Academic libraries have many user categories, complex campus and administrative structures, but a fairly well-defined purpose. Public and school libraries have fewer and more clearly defined user categories and simple site definitions but may have more complex purposes. In addition to traditional informational purposes, public libraries can have recreational missions. Special libraries have unique definitions for all categories: users, site, administrative relationships, use, and purpose.

A library can develop a formal document with its definitions and add it to the end of the contract as an appendix, replacing or enhancing the generic definitions in the license. The following list represents the most common terms defined in licenses. Not all of them must be defined for each license but being aware of common uses and having an understanding of their meanings is important.

- agent
- authentication system
- authorized site
- authorized users
- commercial use
- course packs
- database
- effective date
- electronic reserve
- fee
- intellectual property
- library premises
- licensed materials
- licensed software
- managing agent
- publisher's representative
- remote access
- secure network
- server
- service date
- subscription period
- walk-in users

See appendix D for sample definitions.

E. Basic Rights

A license agreement for an electronic resource should grant certain fundamental rights of use in clear language. Remembering that all rights must be specifically included in the contract, a library should only agree to a license that makes provisions for:

- product access
- product searches
- retrieval of search results
- review and download of information from search results
- printing hard copies of information from search results
- storage of search results in electronic format for a temporary period
- sharing of search results with other authorized users
- inclusion of limited portions of the search results in subsequent works as long as authorship and copyright are noted

If a product's license does not guarantee these basic rights, patrons who are accustomed to having these rights may simply assume that standard use is allowed. Even the best efforts at training, signage, on-screen warnings, and close monitoring by staff cannot assure compliance with such nonstandard usage. If a library is unable to negotiate these basic terms, it should reconsider the acquisition of the product.

Some libraries consider other traditional library use rights to be mandatory, although few insist on every one of these:

- continuing access to or archiving of subscribed materials, if not supplied by the publisher or an intermediary source
- use of the materials for interlibrary loan
- use of the materials in electronic reserves
- use of the materials in electronic course packs
- remote access for distance learners

These rights may be clearly granted in the license. However, they are frequently not mentioned directly but in effect are forbidden by other restrictive terms, such as limitations on distribution and electronic copies. If a library considers these functions to be critical to the value of the product, it must negotiate them into the license before proceeding any further with the acquisition.

F. Obligations

A normal function of a license agreement is to obligate the licensor and licensee to perform specific activities. Both parties should respect these obligations and be prepared to comply with the terms as they are written and agreed to. Obligations applying to a library as licensee may include:

- registration of authorized users in a manner approved by the licensor
- notification of changes to the registered patrons or authorized users' lists

- notification of additions and deletions to the IP range covered by the license
- retention of interlibrary loan, electronic reserve, and course pack records for licensor review
- removal of licensed content from e-reserves or course packs after the end of a course
- immediate notification of any breach of the license
- timely notice of termination of the contract or notice of financial exigency

A library may find some obligations acceptable but not as defined in the license; it may find other obligations unacceptable under any condition. The library should establish policies to handle such situations and in either case will have to negotiate alterations to the objectionable terms or have them removed. Below are some questions a library should ask to establish the licensor's obligations:

- Will the licensee have the right to market the products as advertised and be able to do so without violating the rights of copyright holders?
- How will the licensor provide the product to the licensee (for example, via online access, CD-ROM, or DVD)?
- If access is provided online, which site(s) will be available?
- If the licensor provides the product as a CD-ROM or some other physical object, will it be in working order and free of defects?
- If it is provided online, what is the uptime? What is acceptable performance for the server? Will the licensor maintain backup servers or mirror sites?
- Will technical support be provided? Which browsers, Web tools, etc. are supported?
- How often will the content be updated? Monthly? Weekly? Daily? Will the licensee be notified of content changes and have recourse for significant changes in content?

G. Other Issues

1. Model Licenses

Several national and international organizations have established model licenses to be used during license negotiations between publishers and distributors of electronic products and their customers. One such model, developed by the Council on Library and Information Resources, the Digital Library Foundation, and Yale University Library, is the CLIR/DLF Model License (www.library.yale.edu/~llicense/modlic.shtml). A model used in the United Kingdom is the National Electronic Site License Initiative (NESLI) model (www.nesli.ac.uk). Several publishers are now using it as the basis for their own licenses. In addition, some state/provincial and regional consortia websites have either an adopted model or have one of their own. For example, Consortia Canada, which gathers together consortium directors to promote national site licensing initiatives in Canada, offers a model on its website. Publishers have developed licensing models, too. One example is the draft model license from the Publishers Association and the Joint Information Systems Committee (PA/JISC), which presents a framework for materials supplied in electronic form. Being familiar with these models is good for everyone involved in licensing at the local institutional level. Model licenses are excellent tools for developing institutional guidelines and definitions for licensing.

2. UCITA

The library community has been concerned about recent efforts to weaken copyright fair use allowances in the digital environment and to strengthen licensors' rights under the nonnegotiated license provisions in shrink-wrapped, click-on, and other such licenses through passage of the Uniform Computer Information Transactions Act (UCITA). UCITA is a model code developed by the National Conference of Commissioners on Uniform State Law (NCCUSL) and pushed for adoption at the state level by the Digital Commerce Coalition. NCCUSL is the primary group responsible for the creation and implementation of state purchasing codes. The Digital Commerce Coalition is a loose federation that includes software publishers, as well as media producers. If adopted, UCITA becomes part of a state's legal code governing commercial transactions. The American Library Association (ALA) and several other professional associations, including the American Bar Association, are opposed to UCITA because it supports the legality of nonnegotiable licenses and preempts copyright law governing fair use.

UCITA has the potential to affect the purchase of electronic resources in several ways. Libraries in states that have adopted UCITA must be aware that a click-on or shrink-wrapped license can:

a. block libraries from claiming breach of warranty for "known defects" in products, in effect blocking any claims for restitution.

b. restrict any lending of multimedia products; for example, it may restrict lending of a book with accompanying CD or just of the CD.

c. allow licensors to electronically harvest information on users of their products and the nature of their use without the users' knowledge.

d. remotely disable products without warning or due process or block use for security reasons without interaction with the licensee.

e. change the terms of the contract after the sale and receipt of the product.

Libraries sometimes can guard against such wording in licenses by carefully reviewing them. Click-on licenses are tricky, however, because under UCITA, the license wording on a website can be changed at any time and the changes would be binding. Fortunately, UCITA has failed to be approved in many cases and is unlikely to become law in a majority of states. Several organizations monitor UCITA developments and provide helpful information on their websites. Among them are the Association of Research Libraries (www.arl.org) and the ALA's Washington, DC office (www.ala.org/washoff).

Even libraries located in states where UCITA has not been approved still need to be aware that the law and forum governing a license may be that of a state that has adopted UCITA. If not vigilant in such cases, a library may unintentionally agree to comply with UCITA. When signing agreements with organizations that reside in UCITA states, a library should always include an exclusion amendment stating that the license is not governed by any part of UCITA. Some institutions have added clauses in their purchasing regulations that prohibit staff from agreeing to a UCITA-based license. The website for the American Library Association's (ALA) Washington office contains links to model legal language: http://www.ala.org/ala/washoff/oitp/emailtutorials/ucita.htm.

3. Advocacy Groups

A number of groups concerned with the implications of licensing for electronic information products offer helpful advice on their websites and online discussion groups, which acquisitions and collection development librarians can monitor for valuable ongoing commentary. The International Coalition of Library Consortia (ICOLC) is a grassroots consumer action forum representing all types of libraries through their affiliation with different types of consortia, including specialized, state-wide, regional OCLC-affiliated, and international organizations. The ICOLC holds several meetings annually in North America as well as occasional meetings in Europe. The group has initiated discussion with a wide variety of publishers and vendors of electronic information to encourage them to adhere to model licensing provisions and reasonable pricing models. It has also initiated some multiconsortial purchases, negotiated by a volunteer-sponsoring consortium. The economic clout brought to negotiations and requests for information by this group is significant.

4. Training

Licensing workshops, training sessions, programs, and other learning opportunities are often available through regional or state consortia as well as from national groups like the ARL or the ALA. The ARL has a series of beginning and advanced licensing workshops that are valuable for anyone interested in understanding the licensing process. The workshops are offered at irregular intervals (see www.arl.org/arl/workshops.html for more information). Licensing and the management of electronic resources are currently popular topics and are frequently covered at conferences offered by the ALA and its divisions, such as the Association of College and Research Libraries and the Association for Library Collections and Technical Services.

VI

Consortial Purchasing

Most academic and public libraries in the United States are affiliated with one or more consortia. Normally, at a minimum, a library is a member of both an OCLC regional consortium and a statewide consortium. Library consortia are associations of libraries that form strategic alliances to share funding, resources, technical expertise, and risks. Consortial purchasing has become a very common approach to the acquisition of electronic products and is now one of the most important activities of consortia. Consortial purchasing is advantageous because it brings together a large group of buyers that can approach publishers with greater financial resources than an individual library and can reduce the publisher's business overhead by bringing multiple sales together in a single transaction. A consortium has more clout than an individual library when negotiating licensing terms because it gives the publisher more incentive to change the terms to suit it.

There are many reasons why consortial purchasing has become so prevalent. One important factor is that information in electronic formats is easily shared across broad groups. All users in a consortium have equal 24-7 access to shared electronic resources. In the print environment, consortial purchases (i.e., cooperative collection development) were difficult because delivery of physical items to users at remote sites took time and substantial resources. If an item was not housed locally, users had to wait several days to receive it.

Consortial purchases generally result in reduced costs. However, sometimes the lower costs are actually cost avoidance, not actual reductions in the amount of dollars spent. For example, a library may be paying $1,000 to a certain publisher for subscriptions to ten journals available on the Internet.

The library enters into a consortial agreement that provides access to a group of journals from that publisher if it participates in the purchase with other consortium members. The library now has access to thirty journals for the same dollars they previously paid for ten. The library did not reduce costs but avoided the full cost of the all the journals now available.

It is easier to negotiate favorable licensing terms through consortial purchases for several reasons. The higher the expected revenue, the more willing sellers of electronic products are to change the terms of purchase. Sometimes information providers vary the thresholds for license terms according to the number of libraries participating in the consortial purchase. For example, an information provider may offer continuing ownership rights and interlibrary loan and document delivery options to a large consortium but not to individual institutions. Information providers offer more generous terms to encourage libraries to bring more business to the agreement.

Also, since consortia more frequently become involved in license review and purchase negotiations, consortial representatives have more opportunities to develop negotiation skills, including learning what items are usually acceptable and what items require pressure and leverage to change. They will have a better understanding of areas offering flexibility in the pricing model. Most consortium negotiators are also members of broader groups, such as ICOLC and ALA that provide forums for sharing information on developments in the marketplace—valuable information that describes the strengths and weaknesses of specific licenses in relation to international models.

Another reason for the growing importance of consortia is reduced financial overhead for individual consortium members, since the licensing and purchasing costs are spread among consortial partners. For example, the negotiation of electronic purchases can be a very time-consuming process. Many publishers cannot provide detailed information on current subscriptions, subscription overlap between consortial members, and similar types of data. But within a consortium, an individual or a small group can work to collect this type of information and review and develop acceptable license terms. This is far more cost effective than a noncorsortial approach that has each library repeating the work done at other individual institutions. Consortia offer reduced overhead costs by providing economies of scale for the licensing process.

Many libraries are members of multiple consortia, at least one of which often is a highly organized group with a central office and staff, such as Ohio-Link or an OCLC regional network. Consortia with central organizations exhibit many common characteristics, including:

- funds allocated for a central budget
- incorporation as a governmental agency or a nonprofit corporation

- permanent staff
- decision-making based on input from members

There are also less formal groups with no central organization in which participation is more ad hoc and work is shared among members. A library may be affiliated with several of these groups. These consortia exhibit many common characteristics, including:

- volunteer staff, not permanent employees
- little or no budget for consortial activities
- decisions made independently, then consensus reached at consortial level

A library may establish different relationships with several consortia. It may join a specific consortium just to purchase a single product, or it may have multiple options to purchase the same product within several consortia. Before joining a specific consortium, a library should review its local needs, as those needs should form the basis for determining what type of consortial relationships would be most advantageous. The conditions that influence the type of group in which a library should participate include:

- types of member institutions and the legal requirements of governing bodies
- resources available—both financial as well as personnel
- environment, including current corporate cultures, technical expertise, and technical infrastructure
- expectations and scope
- time frames, including renewal cycles

Different types of consortia do some things better than others and are not necessarily successful at acquiring electronic resources for their members. Some consortia, such as statewide associations and OCLC regional networks, have multiple missions. They might provide broad support for several areas of the library, including cataloging, interlibrary loan, shared systems, and staff training. Their primary function may not be to act as "buying clubs" and due to the wide scope of their mission and constituency, the products they tend to license are of broad general interest. When reviewing an electronic purchase and deciding whether to pursue a consortial purchase, a library should consider what kind of consortium would be best to approach. All types of consortia share certain characteristics, which include:

- value-added services to members
- reduced costs or avoided costs

- effective organization and leadership
- effective lateral and vertical communication
- sustainable organization
- adequate resources (includes funding as well as personnel)
- flexibility of the organization's response to changing markets and needs

It is important to recognize that the process for a consortial purchase is more time consuming than that of a direct purchase, since the decision-making process involves more organizations. Getting all participants to agree and sign off on a purchase will take time. If a product is needed immediately, it is best to pursue directly with the publisher or other supplier and then determine how the purchase can worked into a consortial purchase with the next renewal. An exception to this scenario exists when a consortium already has a product under license, and the license terms allow nonparticipating members to join the purchase at flexible future dates. Some consortial purchases are negotiated to provide open-ended purchase arrangements to members of the group who may not be able to participate in a deal at a specific time but may purchase the product sometime in the future.

The delay in acquiring a product through a consortial purchase is offset by the improved terms of the purchase; if this were not true, group purchases would be rare. The amount of time a purchase takes depends on the purchasing process employed within a consortium. There are as many processes as there are consortial models. Procedures also may vary within a consortium depending on the product being acquired. No hard and fast timetable exists for the acquisition of a given product. Although consortial purchases have many benefits and a significant portion of many libraries' electronic purchases are made in this manner, at times the consortial route is not reasonable. If a product is small and cheap, a library will not want to "spend a dime to save a nickel." If the library has time constraints, it should purchase directly from the supplier. It is worth reiterating, however, that most electronic products are fairly expensive, and the time invested in group purchases usually offers good returns.

A

Sample Nonnegotiable License Agreements

SAMPLE SHRINK-WRAP LICENSE AGREEMENT

1. By making use of the software, which is delivered with this license agreement, the purchaser of the software, also known as licensee, agrees to comply with all the terms and conditions of this license agreement.

2. In consideration of payment of the license fee by the licensee for the software titled "_____ ," _____ the licensor grants a non-exclusive, nontransferable license to the licensee based on the terms and conditions set out below.

3. The licensee agrees that it will use this software solely for its internal purposes and shall not copy, distribute, or transfer to any persons other than employees or students of the licensee. Subject to these restrictions, the licensee may make one copy of the software solely for backup purposes.

4. All title, interest, rights, and copyrights to this software and derivative products shall at all times remain the property of the licensor. Licensee agrees to preserve licensor's property rights.

5. Nothing in this agreement shall be construed as conferring rights to use the software in advertising, publicity, or in other ways use the name of the product or the licensor.

6. Licensee acknowledges that the software is being supplied with documentation "as is" without any accompanying services from the licensor and that any such services and payments as may be required for modifications and enhancements shall be separately negotiated.

7. This agreement shall be governed by the laws of the state of _____ _____.

EXAMPLE OF A CLICK-ON LICENSE

Institution: _____ Sign In as Member or Individual (Nonmember)

The _____ Terms of Agreement

License Agreement

By clicking the "I Agree" button below or signing and returning this Agreement to the Publisher, you agree to be bound by the terms of this License Agreement (the "Agreement"). This Agreement is made and entered into as of the date of your acceptance (the "Effective Date") by and between your company or institution ("Licensee") and _____ _____ ("Publisher").

Preamble

WHEREAS, the Publisher owns and publishes the Licensed Materials (as defined below); and

WHEREAS, the Licensee desires to license the Licensed Materials and the Publisher desires to grant to Licensee the license to use the Licensed Materials in accordance with the terms and conditions of this Agreement. NOW, THEREFORE, the parties hereby agree as follows:

1. Key Definitions

1.1. In this Agreement, the following terms shall have the following meanings:

Agent: A third party appointed from time to time by the Licensee to act on the Licensee's behalf, who may undertake any or all of the obligations of the Licensee under this Agreement, as agreed between the Licensee and the Agent and whom the Licensee identifies to the Publisher in writing. Licensee's appointment of an Agent shall not excuse Licensee from performing its obligations under this Agreement.

Authorized Users:

For academic institutions: ("Academic Institutions") (i) Then-current members of the faculty and other staff of the Licensee (whether on a permanent, temporary, contract, or visiting basis) employed at the Licensee's Premises; (ii) individuals who are enrolled at the Licensee's Academic Institution located on the Licensee's Premises who are permitted to access the Secure Network from within the Library Premises or from such other places where Authorized Users work or study (including but not limited to Authorized Users' offices and homes, residence halls, and student dormitories) and who have been issued a password or other authentication from the Licensee; and (iii) other persons who access the Secure Network from computer terminals within the Library Premises and are permitted to use the Library Premises.

For corporations: Current members of the staff (whether on a permanent, temporary, or contract basis) of the Licensee who are employed at Licensee's Premises and are permitted to access the Secure Network from within the Licensee's Premises or from such other places where such staff undertake their work for the Licensee (including but not limited to Authorized Users' offices and homes) and who have been issued a password or other authentication by the Licensee.

For public libraries: (i) Current members of the staff of the Licensee (whether on a permanent, temporary, or contract basis) who are employed at Licensee's Premises and are permitted to access the Secure Network from within the Library Premises or from such other places where such staff undertake their work for the Licensee and who have been issued a password or other authentication by the Licensee; and (ii) members of the public (patrons) who are permitted to use the Licensee's library and access the Secure Network only from computer terminals within the Library Premises.

Commercial Use: Use for the purposes of monetary gain by any form of exploitation of the Licensed Materials, other than recovery of direct costs by the Licensee from Authorized Users, or use of the Licensed Materials in the course of research funded by a commercial organization.

Course Packs: A collection or compilation of materials (e.g., book chapters, journal articles) assembled by staff members of a Licensee that is an Academic Institution for use by students in a class for the purposes of instruction.

Electronic Reserve: Electronic copies of materials (e.g., book chapters, journal articles) made and stored on the Secure Network by a Licensee that is an Academic Institution for use by students in connection with specific courses of instruction offered by the Licensee to its students.

Licensee's Premises: A single physical location of the institution operated by the Licensee. For Academic Institutions, such a location is a single campus. For corporations, such a location is a single building or corporate campus. For public libraries, such a location is a single building. For avoidance of doubt, if Licensee has multiple physical locations (such as an Academic Institution with multiple campuses) and Licensee wishes to provide access to the Licensed Materials to users at such multiple locations, Licensee must enter into a separate license agreement with Publisher for each such location.

FTEs: An acronym for full-time equivalents and a good faith estimate of the number of Licensee's Authorized Users used to determine the Subscription Fee.

Publisher's Representative: A third party appointed from time to time by the Publisher to act on the Publisher's behalf, who may undertake any or all of the Publisher's obligations under this Agreement, as agreed between the Publisher and the Publisher's Representative.

Library Premises: The physical premises of the library operated by Licensee that is located on the Licensee's Premises.

Licensed Materials: Electronic versions of the issues of *The* _____ _____ published by Publisher from _____, or such earlier date as set by Publisher, to the Effective Date.

Secure Network: A network (whether a stand-alone network or a virtual network within the Internet), which is only accessible to Authorized Users whose identity is authenticated at the time of log-in and periodically thereafter consistent with then-current best practice and security procedures.

Server: The server, either the Publisher's server or a third-party server designated by the Publisher, on which the Licensed Materials are posted and may be accessed.

Subscription Fee: The license fee for each year of the term. The license fee for the first calendar year shall be calculated as set forth on Schedule 1. The Subscription Fee shall be exclusive of any sales, use, value added, or similar taxes, and the Licensee shall be liable for any such taxes in addition to the Subscription Fee.

2. License Grant and Subscription Fee

2.1. The Publisher hereby grants to the Licensee a nonexclusive and nontransferable right to give Authorized Users access to the Licensed Materials via a Secure Network (and via print editions of *The* _____ published by Publisher during the calendar year(s) of the term of this Agreement) for the purposes of research, teaching, and private study, subject to the terms and conditions of this Agreement. Any use of the Licensed Materials not specifically authorized in this Agreement is prohibited.

2.2. The Publisher reserves the right at any time to withdraw from the Licensed Materials any item or part of an item for which it no longer retains the right to publish, or which it has reasonable grounds to believe infringes copyright or is defamatory, obscene, unlawful, or otherwise objectionable.

2.3. The Licensee shall pay to the Publisher the Subscription Fee for the first calendar year of the term within sixty (60) days after the Effective Date. The Licensee shall pay to the Publisher the Subscription Fee for each subsequent calendar year of the term within sixty (60) days after the beginning of each such calendar year. The Agent, if any, will be responsible for processing payment of the Subscription Fee on behalf of the Licensee. If there is no Agent (or if the Agent fails to pay the Subscription Fee to Publisher), the Licensee shall pay the Subscription Fee directly to the Publisher or Publisher's Representative (as specified by Publisher).

3. Delivery of Licensed Materials

3.1. After payment of the Subscription Fee by Licensee, the Publisher shall:

3.1.1. Make the electronic version of the Licensed Materials available to the Licensee from the Server and deliver to the Licensee the print version of all issues of *The* _____ published by Publisher during the calendar year(s) of the term of this Agreement. The Publisher will use commercially reasonable efforts to notify the Licensee and the Agent, if any, in advance of any anticipated specification change applicable to the Licensee's electronic access to the Licensed Materials;

3.1.2. Use commercially reasonable efforts to make the electronic copy of each issue of the Licensed Materials available to Licensee no later than seven (7) days after publication of the printed version of such issue;

3.1.3. Post information on Publisher's website regarding how Licensee can access the Licensed Materials from the Server; and

3.1.4. Use commercially reasonable efforts to make the Licensed Materials available to the Licensee on a twenty-four-hour basis, with the exception of downtimes for routine maintenance and downtimes caused by events beyond the Publisher's reasonable control. In the event of technical problems in the operation of its Server, the Publisher shall take commercially reasonable efforts to remedy any such problems in a timely manner.

4. Usage Rights

4.1. The Licensee may (subject to Section 5 of this Agreement):

4.1.1. Allow Authorized Users to have access to the Licensed Materials from the Server via the Secure Network;

4.1.2. Provide single printed or electronic copies of individual articles to Authorized Users at the request of individual Authorized Users;

4.1.3. Display, download, or print the Licensed Materials for the purpose of training Authorized Users; and

4.1.4. Make such temporary local electronic copies by means of caching or mirrored storage of all or part of the Licensed Materials as are necessary solely to ensure efficient use by Authorized Users and not to make available to Authorized Users duplicate copies of the Licensed Materials.

4.2. Licensee may permit Authorized Users to engage in the following activities in accordance with the copyright laws of the United States and the terms of this Agreement:

4.2.1. Search, view, retrieve, and display the Licensed Materials;

4.2.2. Electronically save individual articles or items of the Licensed Materials for Authorized Users' own research or study;

4.2.3. Print copies of excerpts from the Licensed Materials for Authorized Users' own research or study; and

4.2.4. Distribute copies of individual articles from the Licensed Materials in print or electronic form to other Authorized Users (for the avoidance of doubt, this subclause shall include the distribution of a copy for teaching purposes to each individual student Authorized User in a class at the Licensee's Academic Institution).

4.3. If the Publisher, in its sole discretion, deems it technically feasible, the Publisher shall provide Licensee with access, via the Publisher's website, to the Licensee usage data on the number of articles viewed by Licensee's Authorized Users on at least a quarterly basis. Such usage data shall be for the Licensee's internal use only. Such usage data shall be used and maintained by both parties in a manner consistent with applicable privacy laws and as specified by the Publisher.

5. Usage Restrictions

5.1. Licensee shall not engage in the following activities and shall take all commercially reasonable efforts to prevent Authorized Users from engaging in the following activities:

5.1.1. Removing or altering the authors' names or the Publisher's copyright notices or other means of identification or disclaimers as they appear in the Licensed Materials;

5.1.2. Making print or electronic copies of the Licensed Materials for any purpose (except as authorized by Sections 4 and 6); or

5.1.3. Posting or distributing any part of the Licensed Material on any electronic network other than the Secure Network, including without limitation, the Internet and the World Wide Web.

5.2. The Publisher's prior written consent must be obtained in order to:

5.2.1. Use all or any part of the Licensed Materials for any Commercial Use;

5.2.2. Distribute all or any part of the Licensed Materials to anyone other than Authorized Users;

5.2.3. Publish, distribute, or make available the Licensed Materials, or create any derivative works from the Licensed Materials, other than as permitted in this Agreement; or

5.2.4. Alter, abridge, adapt, or modify the Licensed Materials, except to the extent necessary to make them perceptible on a computer screen to Authorized Users.

6. Course Packs and Electronic Reserve Collections

Notwithstanding anything to the contrary in this Agreement, the Licensee may incorporate articles or portions of articles from the Licensed Materials into printed Course Packs and Electronic Reserve Collections for the use of

Authorized Users in the course of instruction at the Licensee's institution, provided that such Course Packs and Electronic Reserve Collections are not used for any Commercial Use. Each such article or portion of an article shall carry appropriate acknowledgment of the source of such article or portion of an article. Such acknowledgment will contain the name of the author of the applicable article, the title of the article, the phrase "Originally published in *The* _____." Course Packs in nonelectronic, nonprint perceptible form, such as audio or Braille, may also be offered to Authorized Users who, in the reasonable opinion of the Licensee, are visually impaired.

7. Additional Licensee Duties

7.1. The Licensee shall:

7.1.1. Use reasonable efforts to ensure that all Authorized Users are appropriately notified of the importance of respecting the intellectual property rights in the Licensed Materials and of the sanctions which the Licensee imposes for failing to do so;

7.1.2. Use reasonable efforts to ensure that all Authorized Users are appropriately notified of the restrictions placed on Authorized Users' use of the Licensed Materials under this Agreement and take all reasonable steps to protect the Licensed Materials from unauthorized use or other breach of this Agreement;

7.1.3. Use reasonable efforts to monitor compliance and immediately, upon becoming aware of any unauthorized use of the Licensed Materials or other breach of this Agreement, inform the Publisher and take all reasonable and appropriate steps, including disciplinary action, both to ensure that such activity ceases and to prevent any recurrence;

7.1.4. Issue passwords and other access information only to Authorized Users and use best efforts to ensure that Authorized Users do not divulge their passwords or other access information to any third party;

7.1.5. Provide the Publisher with all information requested by Publisher necessary to enable the Publisher to provide access to the Licensed Materials in accordance with its obligation under this Agreement. Should the Licensee make any significant change to such information, it will notify the Publisher not less than ten (10) days before the change takes effect;

7.1.6. Keep full and up-to-date records of all IP addresses used by Licensee to access the Licensed Materials and provide the Publisher with details of additions, deletions, or other alterations to such records as are necessary to enable the Publisher to provide Authorized Users with access to the Licensed Materials as contemplated by this Agreement; and

7.1.7. Use best efforts to ensure that only Authorized Users are permitted access to the Licensed Materials.

8. Ownership

8.1. Nothing in this Agreement shall effect a transfer of copyright rights in the Licensed Materials from the Publisher to the Licensee or its Authorized Users. Subject only to the license granted to the Publisher to use the Licensed Materials hereunder, the Publisher shall retain any rights of copyright in the Licensed Materials that it possessed prior to entering into this Agreement.

9. Representations and Warranties

9.1. The Publisher represents and warrants that (i) it has the right, power, and authority to enter into this Agreement and to perform all of its obligations hereunder; and (ii) the Licensee's use of the Licensed Materials as permitted under this Agreement will not infringe the copyright or any other proprietary or intellectual property rights of any third party.

9.2. The Licensee represents and warrants that it has the right, power, and authority to enter into this Agreement and to perform all of its obligations hereunder.

9.3. EXCEPT AS EXPRESSLY PROVIDED IN THIS AGREEMENT, THE PUBLISHER MAKES NO REPRESENTATIONS OR WARRANTIES OF ANY KIND, EXPRESS OR IMPLIED, INCLUDING, BUT NOT LIMITED TO, WARRANTIES OF DESIGN, ACCURACY OF THE INFORMATION CONTAINED IN THE LICENSED MATERIALS, MERCHANTABILITY OR FITNESS OF USE FOR A PARTICULAR PURPOSE. THE LICENSED MATERIALS ARE SUPPLIED 'AS IS'.

10. Indemnification and Limitation of Liability

10.1. The Publisher shall indemnify and hold harmless the Licensee and its employees from and against any and all losses, liabilities, claims, costs, damages, and expenses (including attorneys' fees and administrative or court costs) arising out of or resulting from third party claims relating to the Publisher's breach or alleged breach of any representation or warranty made by Publisher under Section 9.1(ii). The parties acknowledge that the Publisher has no obligation to indemnify and hold harmless the Licensee from third party claims relating to the use of the Licensed Materials by any unauthorized third party and/or the use of the Licensed Materials in any manner that is not permitted under this Agreement.

10.2. To the extent permitted by law, the Licensee shall indemnify and hold harmless the Publisher, its officers, directors, and employees from and against any and all losses, liabilities, claims, costs, damages, and expenses (including attorneys' fees and administrative or court costs) arising out of or resulting from third party claims relating to (i) the breach or alleged breach of any representation, warranty, or obligation of the Licensee under this Agreement; (ii) use of the Licensed Materials by the Licensee in a manner that is not permitted under this Agreement; and/or (iii) the use of the Licensed Materials by any Authorized User in a manner that is not permitted under this Agreement if Licensee was aware of such unauthorized use.

10.3. EXCEPT FOR THE PARTIES' INDEMNIFICATION OBLIGATIONS UNDER SECTIONS 10.1 AND 10.2, NEITHER PARTY SHALL BE LIABLE FOR ANY CONSEQUENTIAL, INCIDENTAL, INDIRECT, ECONOMIC, SPECIAL, EXEMPLARY OR PUNITIVE DAMAGES INCURRED BY THE OTHER PARTY, EVEN IF THE OTHER PARTY HAS BEEN ADVISED THAT SUCH DAMAGES ARE POSSIBLE.

10.4. EXCEPT FOR THE PARTIES' INDEMNIFICATION OBLIGATIONS UNDER SECTIONS 10.1 AND 10.2, EACH PARTY'S LIABILITY FOR ANY CLAIMS, LOSSES, OR DAMAGES ARISING OUT OF THIS AGREEMENT SHALL IN NO CIRCUMSTANCES EXCEED THE SUBSCRIPTION FEES PAID BY LICENSEE TO THE PUBLISHER UNDER THIS AGREEMENT DURING THE TWELVE (12) MONTH PERIOD IMMEDIATELY PRIOR TO THE DATE ON WHICH SUCH CLAIM, LOSS, OR DAMAGE OCCURRED.

10.5. UNDER NO CIRCUMSTANCES SHALL THE PUBLISHER BE LIABLE TO THE LICENSEE OR ANY OTHER PERSON FOR ANY CLAIMS, LOSSES, OR DAMAGES ARISING OUT OF INTERRUPTIONS IN THE AVAILABILITY OF THE LICENSED MATERIALS NOT WITHIN THE REASONABLE CONTROL OF THE PUBLISHER, INCLUDING WITHOUT LIMITATION, POWER OUTAGES AND FAILURE OF EQUIPMENT OR SERVICES NOT PROVIDED BY THE PUBLISHER.

11. Audit

11.1. The Publisher or its authorized representative shall have the right once per calendar year, at its own expense, to inspect and audit the books and records of the Licensee at the Licensee's offices during normal business hours and upon reasonable notice, to verify the accuracy of the number of Licensee's FTEs.

12. Term and Termination

12.1. The term of this Agreement shall commence on the later of January 1, 2002 or the Effective Date and shall continue until terminated under Section 12.2 of this Agreement. At least sixty (60) days prior to the end of each calendar year during the term, the Publisher shall provide the Licensee with written notice of the Subscription Fee for the subsequent calendar year (the "Notice").

12.2. This Agreement may be terminated under the following circumstances:

12.2.1. If the Licensee fails to pay any Subscription Fee owed by Licensee by the date specified in Section 2.3 of this Agreement or the applicable Notice (whichever is applicable) and fails to remedy such default within thirty (30) days after the date that Licensee receives written notice of such default from by the Publisher, then Publisher may terminate this Agreement immediately;

12.2.2. If either party materially breaches the Agreement and fails to cure such breach within sixty (60) days after the date that the breaching party receives written notice from the other party of such breach, then the non-breaching party may terminate this Agreement;

12.2.3. If either party becomes subject to receivership, liquidation, or similar external administration, then the other party may terminate this Agreement.

12.3. On expiration or termination of this Agreement, all rights and obligations of the parties automatically terminate except that (i) Licensee may continue to make available to its Authorized Users the printed copies of the Licensed Materials that were delivered by Publisher to the Licensee during the term of this Agreement; and (ii) Sections 8, 9, 10, 12, and 13 shall survive.

12.4. On expiration or termination of this Agreement, except as provided under Section 12.3, the Licensee shall immediately cease to distribute or make available the Licensed Materials to any third party and shall remove all Licensed Materials posted on Licensee's Secure Network.

12.5. If Licensee terminates this Agreement under Section 12.2.2, the Publisher shall promptly refund to Licensee a pro rata portion of the Subscription Fee paid by Licensee under this Agreement based on the amount of time remaining in the then-current term.

13. General

13.1. This Agreement constitutes the entire agreement of the parties and supersedes all prior communications, understandings, and agreements relating to the subject matter of this Agreement, whether oral or written.

13.2. Except as provided in this Agreement regarding the Agent, management and operation of the Server, and the Publisher's Representative, this Agreement may not be assigned by either party to any other person or organization, nor may either party subcontract any of its obligations, without the prior written consent of the other party, which consent shall not unreasonably be withheld. Notwithstanding the foregoing sentence, the Publisher may assign this Agreement without the Licensee's consent to any entity that acquires or succeeds by operation of law to all or substantially all of the assets of the Publisher that relate to this Agreement.

13.3. All notices, requests, and other communications hereunder will be in writing and will be sent via U.S. Express Mail, certified mail (return receipt requested), or commercial overnight courier. All notices to the Publisher shall be sent to _____(Publisher's Address) to the attention of the Director of Publications. All notices to the Licensee shall be sent to the address that the Licensee submits to the Publisher pursuant to this Agreement. Either party may notify the other in writing at any time of a change in address for all notices, requests, and other communications hereunder.

13.4. Neither party shall be in default or otherwise liable under this Agreement due to its inability to perform its obligations by reason of circumstances beyond its control (including, without limitation, war, strikes, floods, governmental restrictions, power, telecommunications or Internet failures, or damage to or destruction of any network facilities).

13.5. The invalidity or unenforceability of any provision of this Agreement shall not affect the validity or enforceability of any other provision of this Agreement. In the event that any provision of this Agreement is determined to be invalid, unenforceable, or otherwise illegal, such provision will be deemed restated, in accordance with applicable law, to reflect as nearly as possible the original intentions of the parties, and the remainder of the Agreement will remain in full force and effect.

13.6. Either party's waiver, or failure to require performance by the other, of any provision of this Agreement will not affect its full right to require such performance at any subsequent time, or be taken or held to be a waiver of the provision itself. No term of this Agreement will be deemed waived, and no breach will be deemed excused, unless such waiver or excuse is in writing, is expressly titled waiver of rights, and is executed by the party against whom such waiver is claimed.

13.7. This Agreement shall be governed by the laws of the United States. In the event of a dispute under this Agreement, the parties agree that any dispute that cannot be resolved by the parties shall be decided exclusively by arbitration before a single arbitrator pursuant to the procedures of the American Arbitration Association. The decision of the arbitrator shall be in writing, shall state the reasons for the decision, and shall be final and binding on all parties and anyone claiming through them. Judgment on the award rendered by the arbitrator may be entered in any court having jurisdiction thereof.

13.8. Neither this Agreement nor the relationship of the parties contemplated herein will be deemed or construed to create any partnership, joint venture, or agency relationship between the parties. Neither party is, nor will either party hold itself out to be, vested with any power or right to bind the other party contractually or act on behalf of the other party as a broker, agent, or otherwise.

For Licensees who have not entered into an online license agreement with Publisher: By clicking below, Licensee agrees to be bound by the terms of this Agreement.

For Licensees who have already entered into an online license agreement with Publisher, please print this Agreement, sign and date it below and return it to: Director of Publications, The _____.

Name of Licensee: _____

By: _____

Title: _____

Date: _____

I Agree.

B

The Decision-Making Process for Purchasing Electronic Information Resources

A. THE PROCESS OF DISCOVERY

- What product is being considered for purchase?
- Who can supply the information product; is it available from a single source or from several sources?
- How will access be provided?
- What is the cost, or what are the possible pricing models?

B. WHO NEEDS TO BE INVOLVED?

- Who will negotiate the purchase or license?
- Should the purchase be made through a consortium and, if so, which consortium?
- Does the local business office need to be involved, or if a license is involved, does legal counsel need to be consulted?
- What other library groups, including collection management, systems, or the central computer office, will be affected by the purchase?
- Who will be responsible for setting up local access to the product?
- Who will be responsible for training, if needed, for staff?

C. QUESTIONS INVOLVED IN THE PURCHASING PROCESS

- Has a trial been established to review the product? Will customers be involved?

- Has the product been evaluated for subject content and fulfillment of user needs?
- Is the product compatible with local systems?
- What are the sources of funding? Will alternate titles be canceled to create funds for the new product?
- What are the preferred terms for licensing the product?
- Will the product need to be linked from bibliographic records in the library catalog? Will additional database-specific information be needed to set up a link from a "database list" in the catalog to the product?
- Will the product need to be linked to other online resources?
- Does information concerning the product need to be entered into other electronic resource management systems?
- Is the purchase under time constraints and do these affect other decision points, such as consortial considerations?

C

Licensing Electronic Information Resources

The following is intended to guide the libraries in developing and reviewing purchase proposals and in negotiating contracts or licenses with publishers or vendors of information resources in electronic formats.

BASIC TERMS OF LICENSE AGREEMENTS

A license agreement should state clearly what the licensee is purchasing. The time period for access rights should be explicit. The agreement must assign to the licensor no broader rights than those granted under existing intellectual property laws. For example, the licensor should not be able to claim ownership of the research results obtained from the use of its materials. Such claims would create serious conflicts with intellectual property rights at local levels. A license agreement should clearly define its terms (vocabulary) and employ those terms consistently throughout the document. Use of simple, Standard English is preferred. A license agreement specifies the publishing years covered by the information resource and should require the licensor to notify the licensee in a timely fashion, generally sixty to ninety days, of any changes to the licensed products. A license agreement should include mutual rights to terminate the agreement for just cause and with reasonable due process.

PRICING

Electronic information resources should cost less than the print equivalent and there should be incentives for both the licensee and the licensor to move to electronic-only business models. Additional charges for electronic access must be justified by significant added value in terms of content or access. Purchase of the print or other versions of an information resource must not be required for acquisition of the electronic version. Print copies should be available on a title-by-title basis to the licensee at significant discounts. All pricing information must be explained in detail, including the total purchase costs, how these costs were determined, and even breakdowns for each licensee including pricing model used, subscription costs, and costs for ports or simultaneous users. The licensor should also provide information about the subscription dates and costs, additional costs for backfiles or permanent ownership rights, the price for print subscriptions (if applicable), and how they will handle new titles or removal of content. If backfiles are priced separately, the licensee should expect credits for prior purchases.

PERPETUAL ACCESS TO SUBSCRIBED CONTENT

The licensee should own or have perpetual access guaranteed to the content it purchases. Should the subscription be canceled or if the publisher or vendor ceases to provide access in electronic format, the license terms should ensure continued access to purchased content in the following ways: via online access either through the current site or that of a third party; or via magnetic tape, CD-ROM, or other mutually acceptable electronic format along with the then current software.

SITE

The license must define "site" to include all locations of licensee students, faculty, and staff. Authorized users must be able to use the resources from any geographic location. Clauses that limit access by geographic area (e.g., a five-mile radius of campus) are unacceptable. Many academic institutions provide distance education to students who may be located thousands of miles from a campus. The concept of site limitations based on geographic considerations is challenged by the need to support distance learning.

USERS

Authorized users must be defined to include the licensee's users, including community users, employees, faculty, students, staff, and casual walk-in users.

CONTENT DESCRIPTION

If there are differences between the print and electronic formats of the product, they need to be clearly described in the license agreement. Electronic content should be available before, or no later than, the print equivalent and should include all editorial content found in the print equivalent. Embargoes on the electronic content that go past the release of the print version are not acceptable.

ACCESS

Access should be limited by IP address or domain name. Licensee requests for access by user name and password should also be accommodated. Licensor should agree to cooperate with licensee to implement access control or authentication mechanisms compliant with licensee's authentication infrastructure as the systems are developed and changed.

CLASSROOM SUPPORT

If use is limited by number of simultaneous users, ports, or other factors, adequate access for instructional use (such as library bibliographic instruction sessions) should be supported (e.g., increased concurrent users, more ports) without additional cost.

INTERLIBRARY LOAN

The library must be permitted to use electronic information resources to fill interlibrary loan requests from other institutions. There should be no additional record keeping beyond that required for copyright compliance by the borrowing library.

FAIR USE

Clauses that restrict fair use are unacceptable. A license agreement should protect the commercial interests of the licensor, yet grant user rights (such as fair use, library, and educational rights) that are supported by national law, including the Copyright Act of 1976. The licensor should allow authorized users all normal fair uses of all information for noncommercial educational, instructional, and research purposes, including unlimited viewing, down-loading, and printing. Licensed products must be able to be used to create electronic course packs and must be able to be used for electronic reserves. If any references are made to UCITA, language will be changed or added to make clear that no provision of UCITA shall have any bearing on the license agreement.

LINKING

Licensors should recognize that library users want seamless access to the resources found in their search results—the ability to go from either bibliographic records in online catalogs or citations in established indexing and abstracting services to the full text of the cited content. Products should be designed to accommodate linking from several systems, including bibliographic records in online catalogs, major indexing and abstracting databases, or another third-party linking system. Publishers should support linking directly to the titles and articles in the licensor's products. Use of a licensor's front-end gateway should not be required for access to either journal titles or articles.

Licensee may require support from the licensor to successfully integrate licensed resources into its local system, including the following: first and foremost, a technical contact person and next, a complete list of the journal titles included in the contract as well as ISSNs (print and electronic), the date, volume/issue number of the first electronic issues included in the licensed product, URLs, digital object identifier (DOI) or any other necessary metadata descriptor, the journal title code if it is needed in the URL, and finally an algorithm for computing journal- and article-level URLs. The licensee may find it necessary to use programmatic software to maintain digital object identifiers. If the licensor's site does not permit programmatic access, the licensee will assume permission to run its validation tool for the identifiers that the licensee has assigned to the licensed content. The licensor should give the licensee thirty days' notice if the algorithm changes or if it expects to make major changes to its URLs.

USE STATISTICS

The licensor must agree to provide statistics on the use of the product. The license agreement should stipulate format and delivery schedule for the statistics. It may include the exchange of use data collected by either the licensor or licensee by mutual consent but must not compromise the confidentiality or the privacy of individual users. User data should not be reused or sold to third parties without permission in writing by all signatories to the agreement. The licensor should be willing to generate on a regular and on-going basis both composite use data for the licensee that is system-wide and itemized data for individual libraries. Use data should be at the level of detail required for objective evaluation of product performance and must include title-by-title use of journals. The International Coalition of Library Consortia (ICOLC) "Guidelines for Statistical Measures of Usage" should be followed (see www.library.yale.edu/consortia/webstats.html). Use data may be posted on internal Web sites for the use of member personnel.

RENEWALS

The licensor should provide renewal notices in a mutually agreed to time frame. The license should enable the renegotiation of terms under specified conditions, such as decrease in content or increases in price. The renewal period should allow adequate time, generally sixty to ninety days, for cancellation decisions.

SUBSCRIPTION AGENTS

The licensee must have the option of using the subscription agents of its choice for both print and electronic journals.

TRIALS

The purchasing process should provide an adequate test and evaluation period, generally thirty days, for general access to the production version of the product.

PERFORMANCE

The licensor should provide reasonable assurances regarding the availability and performance of its servers, including redundancy and disaster plans. Performance expectations (such as downtime limits) must be stated along with consequences of not meeting expectations.

ADDITIONAL TERMS NEEDED TO MEET
STATE PURCHASING CODE REQUIREMENTS

Mediation must be the first resort to resolve contract or license disputes.

The agreement should require the licensor to present its product in a form that is compliant with licensee policies and practices designed to comply with the Americans with Disabilities Act.

Library licenses or contracts must be governed by _____ state law, not the laws of other states. If this cannot be inserted into the license's wording, then all clauses regarding governance must be struck from the document. All licensee license agreements conform to current laws of the state of _____ that govern nondiscrimination, arbitration, state obligation, confidentiality, public records, and conflict of interest.

As a matter of policy, a licensee may not enter into an agreement that exposes its member institutions to liabilities arising from third parties who are not signatories of the agreement. Authorized users may not be a party to the license, and licensee cannot take responsibility for the actions of authorized users or any other third party. Also, state law prohibits persons from incurring obligations against the state for which funds have not been appropriated or allocated. These regulations prohibit the state and its agencies from agreeing to hold harmless or indemnify third parties. The licensee shall be liable for claims, damages, or suits arising from the acts, omissions, or negligence of its officers, agents, and employees.

D

Sample Definitions of Terms in License Agreements

agent A third party appointed from time to time by the licensee to act on the licensee's behalf, who may undertake any or all of the obligations of the licensee under this license, as agreed between the licensee and the agent.

authorized users Persons who are authorized to use licensee's library facilities and who are affiliated with licensee as community users, students, faculty or employees, or individuals who are physically present in the library (hereafter defined as walk-ins).

commercial use Use for the purposes of monetary reward (whether by or for the licensee or an authorized user) by means of sale, resale, loan, transfer, hire, or other form of exploitation of the licensed materials. Neither the recovery of direct costs by the licensee from authorized users nor the use by the licensee or by an authorized user of the licensed materials in the course of research funded by a commercial organization is deemed to be commercial use.

course packs A collection or compilation of materials (such as book chapters or journal articles) assembled by staff members of the licensee for use by students in a class for the purposes of instruction.

derivative work A work based on one or more preexisting works such as a modification, enhancement, adaptation, translation, abridgment, or any other form in which such preexisting work may be transformed or incorporated and which, if prepared without authorization from the owner of the copyright or other intellectual property right in such preexisting work, would constitute an infringement of such right.

electronic reserve Electronic copies of materials (such as book chapters or journal articles) made and stored on the secure network by the licensee for use by students in connection with specific courses of instruction offered by the licensee to its students.

fee The fee set out in the license for access to the electronic product, changes which may be agreed to by the parties usually at time of renewal.

intellectual property Any trademarks; issued patents and patent applications; copyrights and copyright registrations and applications; rights in ideas; designs; works of authorship; derivative works; and all other intellectual property rights relating to the licensed materials.

library premises The physical premises of the library or libraries operated by the licensee, as specified in the license.

licensee The customer named in the license, who has authorized the signing of the license, provides access to the licensed materials via its secure network for its authorized users, and is responsible for payments and implementation of the license.

publisher's representative A third party (such as subscription agents or e-journal aggregators) appointed from time to time by the publisher to act on the publisher's behalf, who may execute this license on behalf of the publisher and undertake any or all of the publisher's obligations under this license, as agreed between the publisher and the publisher's representative.

secure network A network (whether a stand-alone network or a virtual network on the Internet) that is accessible only to authorized users approved by the licensee whose identity is authenticated at the time of log-in and periodically thereafter consistent with current best practice, and whose conduct is subject to regulation by the licensee.

server The server, either the publisher's server or a third-party server designated by the publisher, on which the licensed materials are mounted and may be accessed.

subscription period That period nominally covered by the volumes and issues of the licensed material regardless of the actual date of publication.

walk-in users Users from the general public or business invitees who are permitted to access the licensed product through the secure network from computer terminals within the library premises. These designated terminals shall be physically located in libraries or similar physical premises directly controlled by the licensee.

The following are additional sources of sample definitions:

"LibLicense: Licensing Digital Information—A Resource for Librarians" is a website that contains a wealth of valuable information concerning many aspects of licensing and acquiring electronic resources, including an entire section devoted to terms and definitions. Several model licenses provide sample definitions for most of these terms: www.library.yale.edu/~llicense/table.shtml

Licensingmodels.com provides four model licenses that include standard definitions: http://www.licensingmodels.com

The Council on Library and Information Resources, the Digital Library Federation, and Yale University Library have created a model license that contains definitions for many of the above-mentioned items: www.library.yale.edu/~llicense/modlic.shtml

The National Electronic Site License Initiative, sponsored by the Higher Education Funding Councils of England, Scotland, Wales, and Northern Ireland, provides another model license with definitions for many of the above terms: www.nesli.ac.uk/model.htm

Glossary

aggregator A third-party producer that combines the full text of journals or articles originally published by multiple publishers with a common interface or search engine

authentication Verification of identity as a security measure; any process in which a system attempts to validate that users are in fact who they claim to be; IP addresses, passwords, and digital signatures are forms of authentication

bandwidth A measurement of the rate at which data can be transferred; the amount of data flow achieved through Internet connections, which limits speed and complexity of communication, altered by such things as data compression, transmission line speed, or competing traffic

browser Computer software that provides access to the Internet via a communications device; enables users to see Web pages and sites and to communicate with others through the Internet

CGI Common gateway interface

consortium An organization of several libraries joining together as a group for a shared purpose

data sets Raw information in electronic format that is organized by publishers into groups of like information and then made available to external customers

digital archive A long-term storage area in digital format, often on magnetic tape, for backup copies of files or for files that are no longer in active use or high demand

digital library A collection of documents in organized electronic form, available on the Internet. Depending on the specific library, a user may be able to access magazine articles, books, papers, images, sound files, and videos. The concept of digital library is changing constantly and can mean very different things to different people

Digital Millennium Copyright Act (DMCA) Passed in 1998, a major effort to revise copyright law that primarily sought to bring the United States into compliance with international copyright agreements

DOI Digital object identifier

DTD Document type description

DVD Digital versatile disc or digital videodisc

EAD Encoded archival description; encoding standard for archival finding aid

e-book An electronic book; monographic literature that is made available as an individual title via an electronic medium, typically a PDA (personal digital assistant—any battery-powered handheld device that provides digital information management and communications) or the World Wide Web

e-journal An electronic journal; periodical literature that is made available as an individual title via an electronic medium, typically the World Wide Web

EDI Electronic data interchange

federated searching The ability to broadcast a search across many different information products; for example, a search that could be applied simultaneously to the local catalog, several abstracting and index services, and several sources for full text and electronic journals

FTP File transfer protocol

gateway: An adapter inserted into a workstation on the network and connected to the host system by a direct cable or a modem; provides high-speed communication to a mainframe from a network; also enables the network to perform as if it were a mainframe terminal connected to the mainframe

GIS geographic information system; a computer system that contains maps and other types of geographic and demographic information

HD-ROM High-density read-only memory; new storage medium that uses ion beam technology to store data (180 times more than CD-ROM)

ICOLC International Coalition of Library Consortia

interface The link between two different pieces of equipment or the link between two different systems

IP address Internet protocol address

link resolver Software systems that enable automatic links from a source service to appropriate library-specific, full-text copies that the library subscribes to on the Internet; most rely on the use of digital object identifiers and open URLs

local area network (LAN) Workstations linked to each other, typically high-speed communication mechanisms; networked personal computers in a specific work area, that is, a department or an office; also applies to a number of networks in various locations that are connected by a bridge, or a network that is connected to a larger computer by a direct connection or gateway

MARC AMC USMARC archival and manuscript control format

metadata Structured data that describe the attributes of a resource, characterize its relationships, and support its discovery, management, and effective use in an electronic environment

MIDI Musical instrument digital interface

MPEG Moving pictures experts group

NISO National Information Standards Organization

NISTF National Information Systems Task Force

OAIS Open Archival Information System

PDF Portable document format, an Adobe Acrobat file type used commonly for Web-based documents

platform The fundamental level of a computerized system; may refer to the type of operating system (such as Windows, DOS, Unix) or computer (PIII) being used, or the software used to organize and retrieve data

portal Website intended for specific user groups

protocol A set of standardized rules for exchanging information among computers. Different protocols are used for different kinds of communication. For example, the HyperText Transfer Protocol (HTTP) specifies the rules for communication between Web servers and browsers. File Transfer Protocol (FTP) sets the rules for copying files from one computer to another across the Internet

proxy server A server (actual hardware and software) that sits between a client application, such as a Web browser, and a real server; intercepts all or designated requests to the real server, local or distant, to see if it can fulfill the requests itself; if not, it forwards the request to the real server. Proxy servers are frequently used to filter requests, usually for security

remote access: Access to network systems from geographically noncontiguous locations

server Any storage media node on a network, most commonly a file server; a computer program that provides information or services (like e-mail or Web documents) to programs like Netscape

SGML Standard Generalized Markup Language

shareware Public domain software

site license A license agreement that normally allows unlimited use of a product at an individual site

SQL Structured Query Language

TCP/IP Transmission Control Protocol/Internet Protocol; a standard protocol for communications

TIFF Tagged Image File Format

UCITA Uniform Computer Information Transactions Act; a proposed revision to the Uniform Commercial Code (UCC). The UCC is used in most states and makes the principles governing contract law consistent from state to state. UCITA was intended to update the UCC by providing uniform rules for intangible products involved in computer information transactions on the Internet and elsewhere. The Act has not been adopted in most states

usability The effectiveness, efficiency, and satisfaction with which users can achieve tasks using a particular electronic product, including the screen layout and system search capabilities

vertical search engine Provides specialized tools to search specific subject areas; compared to other search engines such as Google, they are distinguished not by how much information they provide but by how little, providing a narrow focus in a specific subject

vortal (vertical portal) A portal focused on a particular market or interest group; in addition to a directory, may also include online services such as free e-mail, shopping, and financial tools

WAP Wireless Application Protocol; a protocol that supports transmission through wireless devices such as personal digital assistants (PDAs) and cellular phones

WCM Web Content Management

XML Extensible Markup Language; technology used in encoded archival description (EAD)

References

ACQUISITIONS AND SELECTION

Berkeley Digital Library SunSite. Digital Library SunSite Collection and Preservation Policy. http://sunsite.berkeley.edu/Admin/collection.html (15 February 2005)

Case Western Reserve University. University Library. Collection Management Policy for Electronic Journals.

Indiana University Bloomington Libraries. Acquisitions, Cataloging, and Collection Development Policies for Electronic Resources. http://www.indiana.edu/~libsalc/policies/e-policies.html (15 February 2005)

International Coalition of Library Consortia (ICOLC). Statement of Current Perspectives and Preferred Practices for the Selection and Purchase of Electronic Information. http://www.library.yale.edu/consortia/2001currentpractices.htm (15 February 2005)

Jewell, Timothy D. Selection and Presentation of Commercially Available Electronic Resources: Issues and Practices. Digital Library Federation, Council on Library and Information Resources, 2001. http://www.clir.org/pubs/abstract/pub99abst.html (15 February 2005)

Okerson, Ann. Electronic Collections Development. http://www.library.yale.edu/~okerson/ecd.html (15 February 2005)

University of Maryland. University Libraries. Collection Development Policy Statement: Guidelines for Selection of Electronic Publications. http://www.lib.umd.edu/CLMD/COLL.Policies/epubguide.html (15 February 2005)

Yale University Library. Guidelines for Shifting Journals from Print to Electronic-Only Access. 2002. http://www.library.yale.edu/ecollections/eonlyguide.html (15 February 2005)

CONSORTIA

The California State University. Systemwide Electronic Information Resources (SEIR). http://www.calstate.edu/SEIR/seir.shtml (15 February 2005)

Coalition for Networked Information (CNI). http://www.cni.org (15 February 2005)

International Coalition of Library Consortia (ICOLC). http://www.library.yale.edu/consortia (15 February 2005)

Queensland University Libraries Office of Cooperation. Consortia Links. http://www.quloc.org.au/consortia_links.html (15 February 2005)

SPARC: The Scholarly Publishing and Academic Resources Coalition. http://www.arl.org/sparc (15 February 2005)

DIGITAL LIBRARY

ARL Digital Initiatives Database. http://www.arl.org/did/index.html (15 February 2005)

California Digital Library (CDL). http://www.cdlib.org (15 February 2005)

Canada's Digital Collections. http://collections.ic.gc.ca (15 February 2005)

Canadian Initiative on Digital Libraries. http://www.collectionscanada.ca/cidl/index-e.html (15 February 2005)

Digital Future Coalition (DFC). http://www.dfc.org (15 February 2005)

Digital Libraries Initiative. http://www.dli2.nsf.gov/dlione (15 February 2005)

Digital Library Federation (DLF). http://www.diglib.org/dlfhomepage.htm (15 February 2005)

D-Lib Magazine. http://www.dlib.org/ (15 February 2005)

University of Michigan. Digital Library Production Service. http://www.umdl.umich.edu (15 February 2005)

ELECTRONIC BOOKS

Association of College and Research Libraries. Western European Studies Section. Electronic Text Collections in Western European Literature. http://www.lib.virginia.edu/wess/etexts.html (15 February 2005)

Bailey, Charles W., Jr. Scholarly Electronic Publishing Bibliography. http://info.lib.uh.edu/sepb/sepb.html (15 February 2005)

California Digital Library. eScholarship Repository. http://repositories.cdlib.org/escholarship (15 February 2005)

Ockerbloom, John Mark. The On-Line Books Page. http://digital.library.upenn.edu/books/ (15 February 2005)

The Oxford Text Archive. http://ota.ahds.ac.uk/ (15 February 2005)

Project Gutenberg. http://gutenberg.net/ (15 February 2005)

The Universal Library. http://serv.ul.cs.cmu.edu/html (15 February 2005)

University of Virginia Library. Electronic Text Center. http://etext.lib.virginia.edu (15 February 2005)

ELECTRONIC JOURNALS

Directory of Open Access Journals (DOAJ). http://www.doaj.org (15 February 2005)
Ejournal SiteGuide: A MetaSource. http://www.library.ubc.ca/ejour/ (15 February 2005)
Harrassowitz. Electronic Journals: A Selected Resource Guide. http://www.harrassowitz .de/top_resources/ejresguide.html (15 February 2005)
Open Journal. http://journals.ecs.soton.ac.uk/ (15 February 2005)

INTELLECTUAL PROPERTY, COPYRIGHT, AND FAIR USE

Association of Research Libraries. Digital Millennium Copyright Act Status and Analysis. http://www.arl.org/info/frn/copy/dmca.html (15 February 2005)
Berkeley Digital Library SunSite. Copyright, Intellectual Property Rights, and Licensing Issues. http://sunsite.berkeley.edu/Copyright/ (15 February 2005)
The Copyright Website. http://www.benedict.com (15 February 2005)
EDUCAUSE. The EDUCAUSE Federal Policy Program. http://www.educause.edu/policy (15 February 2005)
Electronic Frontier Foundation. http://www.eff.org/ (15 February 2005)
Harper, Georgia. Office of General Counsel, University of Texas System. "Copyright Law in the Electronic Environment." http://www.utsystem.edu/ogc/intellectualproperty/ faculty.html (15 February 2005)
International DOI Foundation. Introduction to the Digital Object Identifier System Index. http://www.doi.org/introduction.html (15 February 2005)
International Federation of Library Associations and Institutions (IFLA). Information Policy: Copyright and Intellectual Property. http://www.ifla.org/II/cpyright.htm (15 February 2005)
Stanford University Libraries. Copyright and Fair Use. http://fairuse.stanford.edu (15 February 2005)
The United States Copyright Office. Library of Congress. http://www.copyright.gov/ copyright (15 February 2005)
World Intellectual Property Organization (WIPO). http://www.wipo.int/about-wipo/ en/ (15 February 2005)

LICENSING

Association of Research Libraries. Licensing Electronic Resources. http://arl.cni.org/ scomm/licensing/licbooklet.html (15 February 2005)
Canadian Research Knowledge Network: Licensing Principles. http://www.cnslp.ca/ about/principles (15 February 2005)
Harper, Georgia. Software and Database License Agreement Checklist. http://www .utsystem.edu/ogc/intellectualproperty/dbckfrm1.htm (15 February 2005)

Licensingmodels.com. Model Standard Licenses for Use by Publishers, Librarians, and Subscription Agents for Electronic Resources. http://www.licensingmodels.com/ (15 February 2005)

Principles for Licensing Electronic Resources. http://arl.cni.org/scomm/licensing/principles.html (15 February 2005)

Yale University Library. "Liblicense: Licensing Digital Information—A Resource for Librarians." http://www.library.yale.edu/~llicense/index.shtml (15 February 2005)

LOCAL AREA NETWORKS (LANS)

Local Area Networks Page. http://www.epanorama.net/links/tele_lan.html (15 February 2005)

IT Papers: Networking and Communications. http://www.itpapers.com/index.aspx?ucid=13 (15 February 2005)

Webopedia. Local Area Network. http://www.webopedia.com/TERM/L/local_area_network_LAN.html (15 February 2005)

Wireless Local Area Networks. http://www.doc.ic.ac.uk/~nd/surprise_95/journal/vol2/mjf/article2.html (15 February 2005)

PRESERVATION/ARCHIVAL REPOSITORIES

Consortium of University Research Libraries. Cedars: CURL Exemplars in Digital Archives. http://www.leeds.ac.uk/cedars/ (15 February 2005)

Creative Archiving at Michigan and Leeds: Emulating the Old on the New. CAMiLEON Project. http://www.si.umich.edu/CAMILEON (15 February 2005)

Crow, Raym. SPARC Senior Consultant. SPARC Institutional Repository Checklist & Resource Guide. http://www.arl.org/sparc/IR/IR_Guide.html (15 February 2005)

Digital Library Federation. Minimum Criteria for Archival Repositories of Electronic Journals. http://www.diglib.org/preserve/criteria.htm (15 February 2005)

National Library of Australia. Preserving Access to Digital Information (PADI). http://www.nla.gov.au/padi/ (15 February 2005)

Open Archives Initiative. http://www.openarchives.org (15 February 2005)

Research Libraries Group (RLG). Long-Term Retention of Digital Research Materials. http://www.rlg.org/preserv/ (15 February 2005)

Research Libraries Group (RLG). Preserving Digital Information: Final Report and Recommendations. http://www.rlg.org/ArchTF/index.html (15 February 2005)

Research Libraries Group (RLG). RLG Encoded Archival Description (EAD) Support Site. http://www.rlg.org/rlgead/ (15 February 2005)

NEEDS ASSESSMENT

Brindley, Lynne J. Are They Being Served? http://www.ariadne.ac.uk/issue4/user_services (15 February 2005)

Van House, Nancy A. User Needs Assessment and Evaluation for the UC Berkeley Electronic Environmental Library Project: A Preliminary Report. http://www.csdl .tamu.edu/DL95/papers/vanhouse/vanhouse.html (15 February 2005)

STANDARDS AND METADATA

Association of American Publishers. Metadata Standards for Ebooks. http://www .publishers.org/digital/metadata.pdf (15 February 2005)

Dublin Core Metadata Initiative. http://dublincore.org/ (15 February 2005)

IMS Global Consortium, Inc. IMS Learning Resource Meta-data Specification. http:// www.imsglobal.org/metadata/index.cfm (15 February 2005)

Internet Protocol (IP) Page. http://www.epanorama.net/links/ip.html (15 February 2005)

Library of Congress. Standards. http://lcweb.loc.gov/standards/ (15 February 2005)

The Moving Picture Experts Group (MPEG) Homepage. http://mpeg.telecomitalialab .com/ (15 February 2005)

MPEG Pointers and Resources. http://www.chiariglione.org/mpeg/index.htm (15 February 2005)

MPEG Standards. http://www.chiariglione.org/mpeg/standards.htm (15 February 2005)

National Information Standards Organization. NISO Standards. http://www.niso.org (15 February 2005)

Open eBook Forum (OeBF). http://www.openebook.org/ (15 February 2005)

World Wide Web Consortium (W3C). Metadata and Resource Description. http:// www.w3.org/Metadata/ (15 February 2005)

Additional Resources

GENERAL SOURCES

Bluh, Pamela M., ed. *Managing Electronic Serials: Essays Based On the ALCTS Electronic Serials Institutes, 1997–1999*. Chicago: American Library Association, 2001.

Curtis, Donnelyn, Virginia Scheschy, and Adolfo Tarango. *Developing and Managing Electronic Journal Collections: A How-to-Do-It Manual for Librarians*. New York: Neal-Schuman, 2000.

Johns, Cecily. "Collection Management Strategies in a Digital Environment." *Issues in Science and Technology Librarianship*, 2001, no. 30.

Joint, Nick, and Derek Law. "The Electronic Library: A Review." *Library Review* 49, no. 9 (2000): 428–35.

Jones, Wayne, ed. *E-Serials: Publishers, Libraries, Users, and Standards*. 2nd ed. New York: Haworth Press, 2002.

Kovacs, Diane K. *Building Electronic Library Collections: The Essential Guide to Selection Criteria and Core Subject Collections*. New York, London: Neal-Schuman, 2000.

Lam, Vinh-The. "Organizational and Technical Issues in Providing Access to Electronic Journals." *The Serials Librarian* 39, no. 3 (2001): 25–34.

Lee, Stuart D. *Electronic Collection Development: A Practical Guide*. New York: Neal-Schuman, 2002.

Miller, Ruth H. "Electronic Resources and Academic Libraries, 1980–2000: A Historical Perspective." *Library Trends* 48, no. 4 (spring 2000): 645–71.

Shim, Wonsik, and Charles R. McClure. "Improving Database Vendors' Usage Statistics Reporting through Collaboration between Libraries and Vendors." *College & Research Libraries* 63, no. 6 (November 2002): 499–514.

Smith, Mark. *Neal-Schuman Internet Policy Handbook for Libraries*. New York: Neal-Schuman, 1999.

ACQUISITIONS AND SELECTION

Allison, Dee Ann, Beth McNeil, and Singe Swanson. "Database Selection: One Size Does Not Fit All." *College & Research Libraries* 61, no. 1 (January 2000): 56–63.

Anglada, Luís, and Núria Comellas. "What's Fair? Pricing Models in the Electronic Era." *Library Management* 23, no. 4/5 (2002): 227–33.

Beaubien, Denise M., A. L. Primack, and C. Seale, eds. *Software for Patron Use in Libraries*. Champaign, IL: University of Illinois, Graduate School of Library and Information Science, 1991.

Case, Beau David. "Love's Labour's Lost: The Failure of Traditional Selection Practice in the Acquisitions of Humanities Electronic Texts." *Library Trends* 48, no. 4 (spring 2000): 729–47.

Cline, Nancy M. "Local or Remote Access: Choices and Issues (at Pennsylvania State University)." In *Electronic Access to Information*. Mountain View, CA: Research Libraries Group, 1994.

Cox, John E. "New Models for Serials: Redefining the Serial and the Licensing Environment." *The Serials Librarian* 42, no. 1/2 (2002): 89–99.

Davis, Trisha L. "The Evolution of Selection Activities for Electronic Resources." *Library Trends* 45, no. 3 (winter 1997): 391–403.

Duranceau, Ellen Finnie. "Beyond Print: Revisioning Serials Acquisitions for the Digital Age." *The Serials Librarian* 33, no.1/2 (1998): 83–106.

Faulkner, Lila A., and Karla L. Hahn. "Selecting Electronic Publications: The Development of a Genre Statement." *Issues in Science and Technology Librarianship*, 2001, no. 30 (spring).

Frazier, Kenneth. "The Librarian's Dilemma: Contemplating the Costs of the 'Big Deal.'" *D-Lib Magazine* 7 (March 2001).

Hahn, Karla L., and Lila A. Faulkner. "Evaluative Usage-Based Metrics for the Selection of E-Journals." *College & Research Libraries* 63, no. 3 (May 2002): 215–27.

Hirshon, Arnold, Tom Sanville, Ann Okerson, and David Kohl. "Statement of Current Perspective and Preferred Practices for the Selection and Purchase of Electronic Information." *Information Technology and Libraries* 17, no. 1 (March 1998): 45–50.

Holleman, Curt. "Electronic Resources: Are Basic Criteria for the Selection of Materials Changing?" *Library Trends* 48, no. 4 (spring 2000): 694–710.

Hughes, John Porter. "Outsourcing Electronic Journal Licensing and Negotiation; or, How to Make E-Journal Acquisitions and Licensing Processes as Boring as Ordering Print Journals." *The Serials Librarian* 42, no. 3/4 (2002): 183–89.

Jewell, Timothy D. *Selection and Presentation of Commercially Available Electronic Resources: Issues and Practices*. Washington, DC: Council on Library and Information Resources, Digital Library Federation, 2001.

Johnson, Peggy. "Developing a Local Decision-Making Matrix." *Cataloging and Classification Quarterly* 22, no. 3/4 (1996): 9–24.

Metz, Paul. "Principles of Selection for Electronic Resources." *Library Trends* 48, no. 4 (spring 2000): 711–29.

Miller, Rush. "Shaping Digital Library Content." *Journal of Academic Librarianship* 28, no. 3 (May 2002): 97–104.

Slight-Gibney, Nancy, ed. *Periodical Acquisitions and the Internet.* New York: Haworth Press, 1999.

Smith, Abby. *Strategies for Building Digitized Collections.* Washington, DC: Council on Library and Information Resources, Digital Library Federation, 2001.

Stern, David. "Pricing Models and Payment Schemes for Library Collections." *Online* 26, no. 5 (September/October 2002): 54–60.

Thorton, Glenda Ann. "Impact of Electronic Resources on Collection Development, the Roles of Librarians, and Library Consortia." *Library Trends* 48, no. 4 (spring 2000): 842–56.

ARCHIVING AND PRESERVATION

Barnes, John. "Electronic Archives: An Essential Element in Complete Electronic Journals Solutions." *Information Services & Use* 17, no. 1 (1997): 37–48.

Breeding, Marshall. "Preserving Digital Information." *Information Today* 19, no. 5 (May 2002): 48–49.

Butler, Meredith A. "Issues and Challenges of Archiving and Storing Digital Information: Preserving the Past for Future Scholars." *Journal of Library Administration* 24, no. 4 (1997): 61–79.

Day, Michael William. "Online Serials: Preservation Issues." *The Serials Librarian* 33, no. 3/4 (1998): 199–221.

Dukart, James R. "Electronic Document Archival Dilemma." *e-doc* 16, no. 5 (September/October 2002).

Duranceau, Ellen Finnie. "Archiving and Perpetual Access for Web-based Journals: A Look at the Issues and How Five E-Journal Providers Are Addressing Them." *Serials Review* 24, no. 2 (summer 1998): 110–17.

Feeney, Mary. "Towards a National Strategy for Archiving Digital Materials." *Alexandria* 11, no. 2 (1999): 107–22.

Gertz, Janet. "Selection for Preservation in the Digital Age: An Overview." *Library Resources & Technical Services* 44 (April 2000): 97–104.

Hedstrom, Margaret. "Digital Preservation: A Time Bomb for Digital Libraries." *Computers and the Humanities* 31 (1998): 189–202.

Hodge, Gail M. "Best Practices for Digital Archiving." *D-Lib Magazine* 6, no. 1 (January 2000).

Keyhani, Andrea. "Creating an Electronic Archive: Who Should Do It and Why?" *The Serials Librarian* 34, no. 1/2 (1998): 213–25.

Knutson, Loes. "The Challenges of Preservation in a Digital Library Environment." *Current Studies in Librarianship* 22, no. 1/2 (spring/fall 1998): 56–71.

Lee, Stuart D. *Digital Imaging: A Practical Handbook.* New York: Neal-Schuman, 2001.

Marcum, Deanna. "Digital Archiving: Whose Responsibility Is It?" *College & Research Libraries News* 61, no. 9 (October 2000): 794–97, 807.

Marcum, Deanna, "A Moral and Legal Obligation: Preservation in the Digital Age." *International Information & Library Review* 29, no. 3/4 (September/December 1997): 357–65.

Pitti, Daniel V. "Encoded Archival Description: The Development of an Encoding Standard for Archival Finding Aids." *American Archivist* 60, no. 3 (1997): 268–83.

Smith, Bernard. "Preserving Tomorrow's Memory: Preserving Digital Content for Future Generations." *Information Services & Use* 22, no. 2/3 (2002): 133–40.

Wilson, Lizabeth A. "Coping with the Digital Shift: Archiving and Other Issues to Consider." *The Serials Librarian* 36, no. 1/2 (1999): 137–48.

CONSORTIA

Alexander, Adrian W. "Toward 'The Perfection of Work': Library Consortia in the Digital Age." *Journal of Library Administration* 28, no. 2 (2000): 1–14.

Baker, Angee. "The Impact of Consortia on Database Licensing." *Computers in Libraries* 20, no. 6 (June 2000): 46–50.

Bostick, Sharon L. "The History and Development of Academic Library Consortia in the United States: An Overview." *Journal of Academic Librarianship* 27, no. 2 (March 2001): 128–30.

Button, Leslie Horner. "The Good, the Bad, and the Ugly: Forming Consortia and Licensing." *Library Collections, Acquisitions, and Technical Services* 23, no. 2 (summer 1999): 204–6.

Helmer, John F. "Special Issue: Library Consortia." *Information Technology and Libraries* 17, no. 1 (March 1998): 5–50.

Hiremath, Uma. "Electronic Consortia: Resource Sharing in the Digital Age." *Collection Building* 20, no. 2 (2001): 80–87.

Hirshon, Arnold. "Libraries, Consortia, and Change Management." *Journal of Academic Librarianship* 25, no. 2 (March 1999): 124–26.

Peters, Thomas A. "What's the Big Deal?" *Journal of Academic Librarianship* 27, no. 4 (July 2001): 302–4.

Scigliano, Marisa. "Consortium Purchases: Case Study for a Cost-Benefit Analysis." *Journal of Academic Librarianship* 28, no. 6 (November 2002): 393–400.

Sloan, Bernard G. "Understanding Consortia Better: What Vendors Can Learn." *Library Journal* 125, no. 5 (March 2000): 57–58.

DIGITAL REPOSITORIES

Bertino, Elisa, Barbara Catania, and Gian Piero Zarri. "Metadata, Intelligent Indexing, and Repository Management for Multimedia Digital Libraries." *Fundamenta Informaticae* 47, no. 1/2 (July 2001): 155–74.

Breeding, Marshall. "The Emergence of the Open Archives Initiative." *Information Today* 19, no. 4 (April 2002): 46–47.

Needelman, Mark K. "The Open Archives Initiative." *Serial Review* 28, no. 2 (2002): 156–58.

Peters, Thomas A. "Digital Repositories: Individual, Discipline-Based, Institutional, Consortial, or National?" *Journal of Academic Librarianship* 28, no. 6 (November 2002): 414–18.

Shigo, Kimberly. "Research Libraries Collaborate on DSpace." *Computers in Libraries* 23, no. 4 (April 2003): 8.

Smith, MacKenzie, Mick Bass, and Greg McClellan. "DSpace: An Open Source Dynamic Digital Repository." *D-Lib Magazine* 9, no. 1 (January 2003).

Suleman, Hussein, and Edward A. Fox. "The Open Archive Initiative: Realizing Simple and Effective Digital Library Interoperability." *Journal of Library Administration* 35, no. 1/2 (2001): 125–45.

Tennant, Roy. "Institutional Repositories." *Library Journal* 127, no. 15 (September 15, 2002): 28–30.

Thomas, Sarah. "From Double Fold to Double Bind." *Journal of Academic Librarianship* 28, no. 3 (May 2002): 104–9.

ELECTRONIC BOOKS

Balas, Janet. "Think Like a Patron When You Consider Buying E-Books." *Computers in Libraries* 21, no. 5 (May 2001): 56–58.

Button, Leslie Horner. "Peeking over the Internet's Edge: What's New, What's Coming, and How We'll Use It." *Library Collections, Acquisitions, and Technical Services* 23, no. 2 (summer 1999): 207–8.

Connaway, Lynn Silipigni. "E-Books: New Opportunities and Challenges." *Technicalities* 20 (September/October 2000): 8–10.

Ferguson, Anthony W. "E-Monographs and netLibrary.com: An Alphabetical List of Issues." *The Charleston Advisor* 1, no. 3 (January 2000): 55–58.

Fialkoff, Francine. "E-Books: Coming Faster Than You Think." *Library Journal* 124, no. 12 (July 1999): 75.

Gibbons, Susan. "Ebooks: Some Concerns and Surprises." *portal: Libraries and the Academy* 1, no. 1 (2001): 71–75.

Hawkins, Donald. "Electronic Books: A Major Publishing Revolution." *Online* 24, no. 4 (July/August 2000): 15–28.

Lynch, Clifford A. "Electrifying the Book." *Library Journal* 124, no. 17 (October 15, 1999 supplement): 3–6.

Morgan, Eric Lease. "Electronic Books and Related Technologies." *Computers in Libraries* 19, no. 10 (November/December 1999): 36–39.

Snowhill, Lucia. "E-Books and Their Future in Academic Libraries: An Overview." *D-Lib Magazine* 7 (July/August 2001).

Terry, Ana Arias. "Demystifying the E-Book: What Is It, Where Will It Lead Us, and Who's in the Game? *Against the Grain* 11, no. 5 (November 1999): 18–20.

LEGAL ISSUES/COPYRIGHT

Cheverie, Joan F., and Robert E. Dugan. "The Changing Economics of Information, Technological Development, and Copyright Protection: What Are the Consequences for the Public Domain." *Journal of Academic Librarianship* 28, no. 5 (September 2002): 325–42.

Crews, Kenneth D. *Copyright Essentials for Librarians and Educators.* Chicago: American Library Association, 2000.

Davis, Trisha L. "Legal Issues: The Negotiator's Perspective for Getting to the Heart of the License." In *Virtually Yours: Models for Managing Electronic Resources and Services,* edited by Peggy Johnson and Bonnie MacEwan, 118–26. Chicago: American Library Association, 1999.

Davis, Trisha L. "License Agreements in Lieu of Copyright: Are We Signing Away Our Rights?" *Library Acquisitions: Practice & Theory* 21, no. 1 (1997): 19–28.

Desmarais, Norman. "Copyright and Fair Use of Multimedia Resources." *The Acquisitions Librarian,* 2001, no. 26: 27–59.

Foster, Andrea L. "Academic Library Groups Still Oppose Modified Software Licensing Law." *Chronicle of Higher Education* 49, no. 3 (September 13, 2002), sec. A, p. 36.

Gasaway, Laura. "UCITA and Other Online Contracts." *Information Outlook* 6, no. 10 (October 2002): 44–45.

Gregory, Vicki L. "UCITA: What Does It Mean for Libraries?" *Online* 25 (January/February 2001): 30–34.

Harper, Georgia K. "Copyright Endurance and Change." *EDUCAUSE Review* 35, no. 6 (December 2000): 20–26.

Lemley, Mark A. "Intellectual Property Rights and Standard-Setting Organizations." *California Law Review* 90, no. 6 (December 2002): 1889–1981.

Maynard, Sally, and Eric Davies. "The Cost of Copyright Compliance in Further Education and Higher Education Institutions." *Library Management* 23, no. 4 (2002): 261–62.

Ojala, Marydee Porter. "Preservation, Conservation, and Copyright Infringement." *Online* 25, no. 5 (September/October 2001): 5.

Pike, George H. "The Delicate Dance of Database Licenses, Copyright, and Fair Use." *Computers in Libraries* 22, no. 5 (May 2002): 12–14, 63–64.

Sharp, David K. "Copyright and Licensing in the Electronic Age." *Multimedia Information and Technology* 24, no. 3 (August 1998): 194–97.

Sturges, Paul, et al. "User Privacy in the Digital Library Environment: An Investigation of Policies and Preparedness." *Library Management* 24, no. 1 (2003): 44–50.

Sturges, Paul, Vincent Teng, and Ursula Iliffe. "User Privacy in the Digital Environment: A Matter of Concern for Information Professionals." *Library Management* 22, no. 8 (2001): 364–70.

Wherry, Timothy Lee. *The Librarian's Guide to Intellectual Property in the Digital Age: Copyrights, Patents, and Trademarks.* Chicago: American Library Association, 2002.

Wiant, S. K., and S. McCaslin. "UCITA and Fair Use: A Compatible or Combatable Relationship." *The Serials Librarian* 42, no. 1/2 (2002): 79–87.

LICENSING

Alford, Duncan E. "Negotiating and Analyzing Electronic License Agreements." *Law Library Journal* 94, no. 4 (fall 2002): 621–44.

Allen, Barbara McFadden. "Negotiating Digital Information System Licenses without Losing Your Shirt or Your Soul." *Journal of Library Administration* 24, no. 4 (1997): 15–26.

Berinstein, Paula. "Licensing Images for Use: The Royalty-Free Model—Costs and Legal Aspects." *Online* 22, no. 5 (September/October 1998): 81–84.

Bielefield, Arlene, and Lawrence Cheeseman. *Interpreting and Negotiating Licensing Agreements: A Guidebook for the Library, Research, and Teaching Professions.* New York: Neal-Schuman, 1999.

Bjornshauge, Lars. "Consortia Licensing: Implications for Digital Collection Development." *INSPEL* 33, no. 2 (1999): 116–21.

Blosser, John. "Vendors and Licenses: Adding Value for Customers." *The Serials Librarian* 38, no. 1/2 (2000): 143–46.

Bosch, Stephen. "Licensing Information: Where Can We Go From Here?" *Library Acquisitions* 22, no. 1 (spring 1998): 45–47.

Brennan, Patricia, Karen Hersey, and Georgia Harper. *Licensing Electronic Resources: Strategic and Practical Considerations for Signing Electronic Information Delivery Agreements.* Washington, DC: Association of Research Libraries, 1997.

Buchanan, Nancy L. "Navigating the Electronic River: Electronic Product Licensing and Contracts." *The Serials Librarian* 30, no. 3/4 (1997): 171–82.

Button, Leslie Horner. "The Good, the Bad, and the Ugly: Forming Consortia and Licensing." *Library Collections, Acquisitions, and Technical Services* 23, no. 2 (summer 1999): 204–6.

Cox, John E. "Model Generic Licenses: Cooperation and Competition." *Serials Review* 26, no. 1 (2000): 3–9.

Crews, Kenneth D. "Licensing for Information Resources: Creative Contracts and the Library Mission." In *Virtually Yours: Models for Managing Electronic Resources and Services*, edited by Peggy Johnson and Bonnie MacEwan, 98–110. Chicago: American Library Association, 1999.

Davis, Trisha, and John Joseph Reilly. "Understanding License Agreements for Electronic Products." *The Serials Librarian* 34, no. 1/2 (1998): 247–60.

Duranceau, Ellen Finnie. "License Compliance." *Serials Review* 26, no. 1 (2000): 53–58.

Fisher, Roger, William Ury, and Bruce Patton. *Getting to Yes: Negotiating Agreement without Giving In.* Boston: Houghton Mifflin, 1992.

Guenther, Kim. "Making Smart Licensing Decisions." *Computers in Libraries* 20, no. 6 (June 2000): 58–60.

Harris, Lesley. "Deal-Maker, Deal-Breaker: When to Walk Away." *Library Journal* 125, no. 1 (winter 2000 Net Connect): 12–14.

Harris, Lesley. "Getting What You Bargained For." *Library Journal* 125, no. 7 (spring 2000 Net Connect): 20–22.

Harris, Lesley. *Licensing Digital Content: A Practical Guide for Librarians.* Chicago: American Library Association, 2002.

Johnson, Judy Lenore. "License Review and Negotiation: Building a Team-Based Institutional Process." *Library Collections, Acquisitions, and Technical Services* 23, no. 3 (fall 1999): 339–41.

Kaye, Laurie. "Owning and Licensing Content: Key Legal Issues in the Electronic Environment." *Journal of Information Science* 25, no. 1 (1999): 7–14.

Keyhani, Andrea. "Coping With the Digital Shift: Four of the Thorniest Issues." *The Serials Librarian* 36, no. 1/2 (1999): 149–62.

Klugkist, Alex C. "LIBER Licensing Principles for Electronic Information." *Journal of Academic Librarianship* 26, no. 3 (May 2000): 199–201.

Okerson, Ann. "The Transition to Electronic Content Licensing: The Institutional Context in 1997." In *Technology and Scholarly Communication*. Berkeley, CA: University of California Press, 1999.

Schmidt, Karen A. "Licensing: Pitfalls and Protection for the Collection." In *Virtually Yours: Models for Managing Electronic Resources and Services*, edited by Peggy Johnson and Bonnie MacEwan, 111–17. Chicago: American Library Association, 1999.

Schottlaender, Brian. "The Development of National Principles to Guide Librarians in Licensing Electronic Resources." *Library Acquisitions* 22, no. 1 (spring 1998): 49–54.

Schulman, Sandy. "The Semantics of Site License Agreements." *Information Today* 15, no. 1 (January 1998): 42.

Soete, George J. *Managing the Licensing of Electronic Products*. SPEC Kit 248. Washington, DC: Association of Research Libraries, 1999.

Srivastava, Sandhya D. "Licensing Electronic Resources." *The Serials Librarian* 42, no. 1/2 (2002): 7–12.

Terry, Ana Arias. "Legally Speaking from Concept to Working Model: Generic Licenses Effort for E-Resources Provide More Than Flexible Templates." *Against the Grain* 12, no. 1 (February 2000): 57–58.

Webb, John P. "Managing Licensed Networked Electronic Resources in a University Library." *Information Technology and Libraries* 17, no. 4 (December 1998): 198–206.

REVIEW SOURCES

The Charleston Advisor: Critical Reviews of Web Products for Information Professionals. Denver: The Charleston Company, 1999: http://www.charlestonco.com/ (3 December 2003).

"*ChoiceReviews.Online.*" Chicago: American Library Association. Association of College and Research Libraries, 2000: http://www.choicereviews.org (3 December 2003).

Chronicle of Higher Education "Information Technology Resources." Washington, DC: Chronicle of Higher Education, 1990: http://chronicle.com/infotech (25 November 2003).

Electronic Resources Review. Bradford, West Yorkshire: MCB University Press, 2000: http://www.emerald-library.com (25 November 2003).

Information Today. Medford, NJ: Learned Information, Inc., 1984: http://www.infotoday.com/it/itnew.htm (25 November 2003).

Library Journal. Chicago: American Library Association, 1976: http://libraryjournal.reviewsnews.com (25 November 2003).

ONLINE. Wilton, CT: Information Today. Medford, NJ, 1997: http://www.infotoday.com/online/default.shtml (25 November 2003).

Online Information Review. Bradford, West Yorkshire: MCB University Press, 2000: http://www.emerald-library.com (2 December 2003).

School Library Journal. New York: Reed Business Information, 1961: http://slj.reviews news.com (2 December 2003).

Teacher Librarian. Seattle: Rockland Press, 1998: http://www.teacherlibrarian.com (2 December 2003).

STANDARDS

Braid, Andrew. "Improved Access for End-Users through the Use of Standards." *Interlending & Document Supply* 28, no. 1 (2000): 8–14.

Day, Neil. "MPEG-7: Solutions for Rich Content Management." *Online* 25, no. 5 (September/October 2001): 50–53.

Harris, Patricia R. "Why Standards Matter." *portal: Libraries and the Academy* 1, no. 4 (2001): 525–29.

Moen, William E. "Interoperability for Information Access: Technical Standards and Policy Considerations." *Journal of Academic Librarianship* 26, no. 2 (March 2000): 129–32.

Parker, Dana J. "Fifteen Flavors of DVS," *Emedia* 13, no. 6 (June 2000): 88.

Paul, Sandra K. "Update on Standards from a Global Perspective." *Library Hi Tech* 18, no. 7 (2001): 1.

USER NEEDS ASSESSMENT

Andrews, Susan. "Meeting End User Needs in the Electronic Universe: A Dialogue." *The Serials Librarian* 36, no. 1/2 (1999): 247–51.

Belefant-Miller, Helen, and Donald W. King. "A Profile of Faculty Reading and Information-Use Behaviors on the Cusp of the Electronic Age." *Journal of the American Society for Information Science and Technology* 54, no. 2 (2003): 179–81.

Bosch, Stephen J., Chris Sugnet, and Dora Biblarz. *Guide to User Needs Assessment for Integrated Information Resource Management and Collection Development.* Chicago: American Library Association, 2001.

Breeding, Marshall. "Strategies for Measuring and Implementing E-Use." *Library Technology Reports* 38, no. 3 (May/June 2002): 1–70.

Crawford, Gregory A. "Issues for the Digital Library." *Computers in Libraries* 19, no. 5 (May 1999): 62–64.

Jie, Tian, and Sharon Wiles-Young. "The Convergence of User Needs, Collection Building, and the Electronic Publishing Market Place." *The Serials Librarian* 38, no. 3/4 (2000): 333–40.

MacEwan, Bonnie. "Understanding Users' Needs and Making Collections Choices." *Library Collections, Acquisitions, and Technical Services* 23, no. 3 (1999): 315–20.

Reed, Bonnie. "Information Needs and Library Services for the Fine Arts Faculty." *Journal of Academic Librarianship* 27, no. 3 (May 2001): 229–33.

Spanner, Don. "Border Crossings: Understanding the Cultural and Informational Dilemmas of Interdisciplinary Scholars." *Journal of Academic Librarianship* 27, no. 5 (September 2001): 352–60.

Townley, Charles Thomas, and Leigh Murray. "Use-Based Criteria for Selecting Electronic Information: A Case Study of Six University Libraries." *Information Technology and Libraries* 18, no. 1 (March 1999): 32–39.

Westbrook, Lynn. "Analyzing Community Information Needs: A Holistic Approach." *Library Administration & Management* 14, no. 1 (winter 2000): 26–30.

Westbrook, Lynn. *Identifying and Analyzing User Needs: A Complete Handbook and Ready-to-Use Assessment Workbook with Disk.* New York: Neal-Schuman, 2001.

Westbrook, Lynn, and Steven A. Tucker. "Understanding Faculty Information Needs: A Process in the Context of Service." *Reference & User Services Quarterly* 42, no. 2 (winter 2002): 144–48.

Xie, Hong, and Colleen Cool. "Ease of Use versus User Control: An Evaluation of Web and Non-Web Interfaces of Online Databases." *Online Information Review* 24, no. 2 (2000): 102–15.